Praise for *Confession*

"Glenn Belverio has a devastatingly urban eye. An ultrahip arbiter of style, he commands the fine line between fashion and flash. He is a superb guide to the underworld of earthly delights."
—Bestselling author and culture critic Camille Paglia

"*Confessions from the Velvet Ropes* is like a surreal mash-up of *Party Girl* and *Apocalypse Now*, or maybe *Please Kill Me* and *Night of the Living Dead*. It's packed with absurdly juicy war stories from the velvet gold mine of New York clubland, down and dirty yet screamingly funny tales from the door-bitch jungle, full of crazed revelers, wasted starlets, fashion pimps, and sex behind the ice machine. Brilliant stuff."
—Rob Sheffield, *Rolling Stone*

"Belverio's corrosive humor cuts to the quick of the social body. He has Wildean wit and a superb sense of the absurd. His wry, entertaining writing style puts you right at the center of any V.I.P. event. This is gonzo journalism at its most compelling, full of celebration and sharp insight."
—Bruce Benderson, author of *The Romanian: Story of an Obsession* and *User*

"Imagine a literary cocktail composed of equal parts Suzy Menkes, Truman Capote, and Jacqueline Susann, then add a twist of New York street smarts and the result is Glenn Belverio. If David Sedaris wasn't a virgin, he might write something like Belverio."
—Bruce LaBruce, filmmaker and author of *The Reluctant Pornographer*

CONFESSIONS FROM

The

VELVET ROPES

THE GLAMOROUS, GRUELING LIFE
of THOMAS ONORATO,
NEW YORK'S TOP CLUB DOORMAN

GLENN BELVERIO

ST. MARTIN'S GRIFFIN   NEW YORK

www.stmartins.com

Book design by Jonathan Bennett

Library of Congress Cataloging-in-Publication Data

Belverio, Glenn.
   Confessions from the velvet ropes : the glamorous, grueling life of Thomas Onorato, New York's top club doorman / Glenn Belverio.—1st ed.
      p. cm
   ISBN-13: 978-0-312-35459-6
   ISBN-10: 0-312-35459-2
      1. New York (N.Y.)—Social life and customs.   2. Nightclubs—New York (State)—New York.   3. Onorato, Thomas.   I. Onorato, Thomas.   II. Title.

F128.55.B45 2006
974.7'1—dc22

2006041719

First Edition: July 2006

10 9 8 7 6 5 4 3 2 1

In memory of my friend Robert Young (1963–2005).
New York will never be the same without him.

ACKNOWLEDGMENTS

First and foremost, I'd like to thank Thomas Onorato for all his many, many hours of help and commitment (which, in the Italian-American tradition, involved lots of dramatic yelling and good-natured, back-and-forth insults) and all his club and music scene wisdom. Also my friend Michael Schmidt, for all the hedonistic and intellectually stimulating nights out in New York. Even when the sun comes up and we're too drunk to stand, we still manage to roll out the bon mots and the fashion and rock world anecdotes. . . . and Martin Belk (we both gave up Jägermeister for writing).

I would also like to thank Constantino Belverio (my Dad), Bruce Benderson (for all his support and valuable advice over the years), Bruce LaBruce (for being the Michael to my Donald), Camille Paglia (for all of her support, inspiration and hilarious notes and e-mails over the years), Rebecca Voight (my wonderful editor in Paris, who has always believed in my writing—thank you for all the encouragement and inspiration), Kelly Cutrone (someday we'll get married), Mark Simpson (I still have that incriminating photo of you enjoying *Ab Fab*), my fabulous editor, Becki Heller (my next book will be a collection of obscure and dated film and Broadway musical references), my agent Doug Stewart at Sterling Lord (for all his terrific advice), Michael T. (glamour incarnate), Kenny Kenny (Shiva on earth, who's proved that people can change), Derek Neen (for his great sense of humor and charm, and all the walks down East Village memory lane), Marc Benecke (a thrill to meet the Godfather of the velvet ropes), Justine D., Larry Tee, The MisShapes, T. C. Conroy, Sarah Lewitinn, Anthony Haden-Guest, Liberation, Lauren Pine, Lyle Derek, Ronnie Cutrone, Dennis Stansbury (because you are you), Vaginal Davis (always an inspiration), Laurie Pike (for getting me into this whole writing business in the first place), Diane Pernet (who's probably attending fashion week in Antarctica or the Republic of Congo right now), Rupert Goldsworthy (you broke the rules), Duncan Elliott (aka Brenda Sexual), Corey Sabourin (Fidel is always on the VIP list), Aric Chen, Patty Powers, Scot D. Ryersson and Michael Orlando (authors of the amazing *Infinite Variety: The Life and Legend of the Marchesa Casati*), Damion Matthews (my fellow Vreelandite), Mina Estevez (pass the bitter melon), Yt Orlando (who's always on the right side of the ropes), Anouche Wise, Joselle Yokogawa, Aaron Rassmussen, Kevin Lee and Tomoko Kikuchi (I miss you guys!), Ken Siman, Rex Reed (for *People are Crazy Here*), Jay Blotcher and the Ghost of Jackie Susann.

ACKNOWLEDGMENTS

THOMAS ONORATO

First and foremost I would like to thank Glenn Belverio for truly making this book what it is. You are brilliantly intelligent and always witty. Who would have thought after years of calling you my "mentor," I would get the honor of working with you as a collaborator. I must also thank the amazing team around us that helped make this book possible, including our editor Rebecca Heller, Doug Stewart, and Franz Gaijin. I would like to thank some near and dear friends and advisors who were kind enough to hold my hand throughout this process, including my loving mom Toni, my life coach T. C. Conroy, the amazing Kirsten "Skip" Major, my colleague Max Wixom, Kelly Cutrone, whose words convinced me to do this book, and the omniscient Martin Belk.

There are many people who contributed to this book or helped me become this person, and I am grateful to you all. I will do my best to thank all of you, but if I forget anyone, please know that I value all your love and support over the years. Firstly, I must thank Squeezebox creator Michael Schmidt, who gave me my start in this business and taught me the ins and outs of club land, and that the real power is located behind the scenes. Many thank yous must also go to Patrick Briggs, Mr. Tim, Lauren Pine, Misstress Formika, Miss Guy, Sherry Vine, Ronnie, Don Hill, Lisa, Justin Bond, Michael Cavadias, The Motherfuckers' "man-lady" Michael T., "lady woman" Justine D., Johnny T., and Georgie Seville, The MisShapes Geordon, Leigh, and Greg, Dino Minelli, Sarah Lewitinn, Tricia Romano,

Sia Michel, Bruce Tantum, Trenton Straube, Gregory T. Angelo, Les Simpson, Roger, Mauricio and everyone at MAO PR, my "it" girl Autumn Binion, Abby Ehmann, Brian Damage, Whitey, Paul Devitt, Chris and everyone at Coral Room, Kenny Kenny, Derek Neen, Marc Benecke, Larry Tee, Conrad Ventur, Spencer Product, Joey, Zoe, Emilia and everyone at Nadine Johnson, Mickey Boardman, Drew Elliott, Richie Rich, Traver Rains, Aimee Philips, Macky Dugan and everyone at Heatherette, Tommy Saleh, Mandy Brooks and everyone at Tribeca Grand, "Spiky" Phil Meynell, David Pianka, Josh Houtkin, Cowboy Dave, Josh Menendez and Club Revolver, George, Mike, Christine, Tim, Nacona and everyone at B-Rude, Angela Shore, Brian Philips, Michael Goodstein, Jerry Kolber and Brian Suarez, Nicky and everyone at Crobar, Tom, Alejandro and everyone at GBH, Michael Matula and Mudhoney, Theodora Sopko, Zach Eichman, Dylan Pass, Jet, James Vincent and Pretty Pretty, Christopher Crawford and Angela Deane, Alex Resto, Luisa Lam, Derrick Maddox, Lyle Derek, the lady Jessica Matlin, Faran Krentcil, the fearless Joseph Janus, Patricia Kennedy, Tom Renaud, Bob Gruen. Eddie Newton, Alexander Thompson, Sean Dack, Tina and Arlene of Fifi Bear, Merlin Bronques, Scott Meriam, Jimmy James, Damien and The Explosion, Melissa Burns, George McAvoy, Richard Tremblay, Craig Robinson, Sean Wicker, Andrew Caldwell, Maro Hagopian Caleb McLoud, Peter at Dior Homme, everyone at Marc by Marc Jacobs, A La Disposition, Sophia Lamar, Zaldy, Zoe Bruns, Joseph McElroy, Anja Brinich, Adrienne Belk, the

ACKNOWLEDGMENTS

Imaginary Socialite, Tanya Pacht, Michael Akers, Peppermint Gummybear, Theo Kogan, Ron M, Miranda Moondust, Haley Hottpink and "The Duchess of RAZZLE DAZZLE" herself, Duch. My lovely, unique and original friends William Murphy, Edward Bottger, Hope Miller, Jesse Murray, Jessica Honikman, Chezza Zoeller, Tim McLusky, Demetre D., Virginia Farley, Rita Costa, Andrea Lawn, Jessica Smith.

Due to timing, limitations, and different constraints, certain door people that I learned from and that inspired me are not featured in this book extensively, including my good friend Connie "Girl" Flemming, the legendary Kitty Boots, Darrell Elmore, Mike Ford, and Gilbert Stafford.

I would not be who I am and have my "lust for life" without the influence and teachings of some of my longtime idols, including David Bowie, Siouxsie Sioux, Kate Bush, Diana Vreeland, Andy Warhol, Edie Sedgwick, Candy Darling, Richard Martin, Stephen Sprouse, Vivienne Westwood, The Clash, Tom Wolfe, Mark Simpson, Bruce LaBruce, Disco 2000, and Visionaire. Lastly, I must give my due to all "the children" of the night, the "it" girls, rock and roll boys, DJs, gays, glamazons, queens, trannies, freaks, fashionistas, and legends that go out and make all these parties so amazing. You all inspire me and I would have never started doing this job eight years ago if it were not for every one of you. Don't stop now kiddies, we're just getting started!

CONFESSIONS FROM *The*
VELVET ROPES

INTRODUCTION

Down in dawntown there's a club I wanna take me to.
—RICHARD HELL AND THE VOIDOIDS

One of my earliest memories from the year I moved to New York is of a wonderfully dilapidated club called The World. Located at the corner of East Second Street and Avenue C, The World was the sort of place you risked your life to get to in those pregentrification times—and it was worth it. On one particular night in 1987, a fabulous transsexual named International Chrysis—now deceased—was performing in the downstairs Chandelier Room. Clad in a sheer, sparkly bodysuit and towering stilettos, Chrysis vamped around the intimate space with the presence of a Babylonian goddess, drawing cheers and applause from the worshipful crowd. When a duo called The Pop Tarts—who later founded the influential World of Wonder production company—took the floor-level stage after Chrysis was finished and said into the mike "We *love* this club," they were definitely preaching to the night-crawling choir.

RuPaul—well before she was a household name—was imperiously stalking the room wearing a corset, with a jumble of words and symbols scrawled on her face in eyeliner. The club kids, who dressed in outfits that would have made Salvador Dali blush, were just starting to find their nightlife niche, and, along with numerous artists, writers, and full-time layabouts, they came to The World to drink, gossip, and fish for compliments. I really felt I was a part of something exciting and unique; that the new center of civilization was in this room, located in a cavernous, dank club, and it was only a matter of time before the rest of the world outside of The World realized this.

Around this time there was also Savage—a tacky, 'seventies-style, mirror-covered discothèque that was invaded by the new guard of cool every Tuesday night. I witnessed performance artist Leigh Bowery make an infamous appearance there, with illuminated light bulbs protruding from his ears, and the club kids copied his fiendish ensembles thereafter for the next five years and longer. There were nights in the VIP room at Tunnel, where I remember seeing a well-behaved Ozzy Osbourne, a decade before he became a burnt-out spectacle. I also met Divine there, who was out of drag and loudly holding court, and watched naked transsexuals stage wrestling competitions. Diane "Queen of the Night" Brill's mammoth breasts were omnipresent, and the frenzied ten-P.M.-to-midnight open bar became a blood sport for impoverished young alcoholics. A year or two later there was Larry Tee's Love Machine at the Underground, where RuPaul was often drunk and chasing nearly-naked hunks across the dance floor. The Pyramid Club on Avenue A was an institution where demented performers with names like Hapi Phace, Sister Dimension, and Tabboo! served up cocktails of wicked satire and an irreverent approach to drag. New York City was, as the Nina Hagen song goes, the hottest place.

By 1994 this style of nightlife had mainly run its course: the Pyramid queens had run out of steam, the club kids were destroying themselves with heroin and Special K, Diane Brill had apparently fled to Germany, and thousands of gifted people died of AIDS—including Leigh Bowery who passed away on the last day of that year. It was time for something new, something that brought back what was great about what was old. Michael Schmidt's Squeezebox combined the 'seventies punk energy of the Mudd Club and CBGB's with the maverick New York drag queen sensibility of the 'eighties and drew a crowd of beautiful freaks every Friday night at a Soho club called Don Hill's. Riding on the success of that party, a few years later Michael also launched a Wednesday night rock 'n' roll soiree called Lust for Life at a club called Life on Bleecker Street. It was there that I met Thomas Onorato.

I had recently returned from a retrospective of my film and video work that was screened at the Institute of Contemporary Art in London, and I was laughing with my friend Martin Belk about the chaos we had again stirred at last Friday's installment of Squeezebox. Martin and I were notorious for getting shit-faced drunk there every week, and at about 3:50 A.M., we would storm the dance floor arm in arm, like Laverne and Shirley on crack. We then proceeded to slam dance into everyone there, sending half-finished drinks, chairs, and people careening in every direction, and inadvertently inflicting bruises and bloody noses.

"I *love* it when they do that!" Don Hill, the owner of the club, would say every week. "It clears out the club so we can turn off the lights and all go home!" As we were recounting our tale of carnage to a friend who had luckily left the club early that night, Thomas came walking over and Martin introduced him as one of the brand new promoters for Squeezebox. As it turned out, Thomas already knew of me. "I watch you on the Sundance Channel every Sunday morning," he informed me excitedly. Not having cable, it took me a few moments to realize that he was referring to a documentary I was featured in about independent filmmakers—directed by actress Illeana Douglas—that was being repeated on a regular basis. I suppose I should mention that I appear in the film as my former performance artist persona, a drag queen named Glennda Orgasm . . . but I won't.

After that night, I soon began seeing Thomas working at the door of Squeezebox, wielding a guest list and a formidable glam-rock attitude. Naturally, he was courteous and friendly to me and everyone else who also had a ridiculous stage name, but he also had an imperious, impatient streak in him. On one occasion, I witnessed him make a young woman cry. She had approached him during an especially busy night and mentioned she had met him recently at a party. "I don't have time to talk to you now," he said curtly, throwing his hand back in a dismissive gesture and barely giving her the once-over. The weeping girl, a DJ and club promoter named Justine D., later became good friends with Thomas as well as one of his bosses at the successful Motherfucker rock 'n' roll party. "I used to call him 'that door monster' before we hired him," she often tells people.

After Squeezebox ended, I went on a hiatus from New York nightlife and began accepting journalistic assignments in Asia and Europe. I kept in touch with Thomas but felt too jaded to frolic with the twenty-somethings who populated many of the clubs where he worked the doors. Then, last winter, Thomas invited me to a press screening of Woody Allen's wonderful *Melinda and Melinda* and afterwards we inspected Christo's Florida orange tarps—"The Gates"—in snow-covered Central Park. It was then that he informed me of the idea for this book and I decided that I should be the one to write it. *It'll get me out of the house,* I reasoned. So I plunged back into the New York club scene, but this time as an observer rather than a participant (for the most part—I still have a pulse, after all) and also listened to all the crazy stories from the club, fashion, and celebrity-party worlds to which Thomas acts as a gatekeeper.

Think of this book as a cautionary tale, a guidebook, an excuse to go out, an excuse *not* to go out. Think of it as a social X-ray that reveals the pleasure principle of today's partygoers and all the well-oiled, working parts of the doorman. And if you do decide to venture out in the hopes that you will make it past Checkpoint Charlie—crossing the wall that separates your dreary existence from a land of hedonistic abandon—bear in mind the Thomas Onorato mantra: "I don't care what kind of look you work, just work one."

Glenn Belverio
New York, 2005

1 .

I got a date with the night.
—YEAH YEAH YEAHS

Hi." This is a message for Thomas Onorato. My name is
Sarah Goreman and I'm the fashion editor for Irish *Márie
Claire* magazine." The shrill, nasally voice that is being emit-
ted from Thomas's answering machine has the aural appeal of
a car alarm. Thomas rolls his eyes as he applies a layer of Shu
Uemura pancake foundation. *There's no such thing as an Irish
Marie Claire,* he says to himself. "And I'm calling to find out if
I can get on the list tonight for the Cirque du Soleil party at
The Roxy. I'd like to bring the photo editor from *Ocean Drive*
magazine, his two assistants, Omarosa's stylist—" Thomas
throws his makeup sponge down in disgust at the mention of
the C-list celebrity name. He stomps over to the phone and
picks it up.

"Hi, this is Thomas and I'm very sorry, but the guest list is
closed for the night." He tries to sound sweet, but after dealing
with dozens of calls like this tonight, he's more than a bit
exasperated—and late for a meeting with the club's staff. "And

just so you know—it's not a party for Cirque du Soleil, it's Motherfucker's fifth anniversary. The party has a circus *theme*." He hangs up and punches in the number for his car service, hoping that the ten minutes it will take the car to get there will be enough time for him to apply his eye makeup—just a dab to complete his rocker chic look—and get dressed.

Thomas arrives at The Roxy thirty minutes late, which, in club time, is about an hour early. Maura, an assistant to one of the party's organizers, is standing by the coat check counter opening up boxes that contain CD samplers and copies of *Paper* magazine, which will be distributed to the party's attendees. She is dressed in a vintage 'fifties black swimsuit and a yellow bolero jacket. "Hi Maura," Thomas says. "Love the look." He begins organizing the various guest lists for the evening. "Are the midget, er, 'vertically challenged' go-go dancers here yet?" he asks.

"I think I saw a mini Alice Cooper over by the ice machine a few minutes ago, but I'm not positive," she tells him. "I was up late last night working on a paper, so sometimes I imagine things when I'm overtired." Maura is studying "feminist geography" at the New School and is working on a thesis about the "gender and geography of dance floors." At one point she sets down a stack of CDs, whips out a notepad, and reads a passage from her thesis. "Motherfucker has always appeared to me to be inclusive to all things feminine. At any given moment I could look around the room and see many bodies parading around in short skirts, high heels, and fabulous wigs—yet this scene never seems defined by biology in the decision of who 'gets to wear the pants.'"

"That's fab, doll!" Thomas enthuses. "It puts me in mind of the time Susan Sontag showed up at Jackie 60. Apparently Betty Page and bondage were on her menu that week."

Tonight is the fifth anniversary of Motherfucker, a very successful, multisexual party held at changing venues, that blends timeless rock 'n' roll attitude, androgyny, retro cheekiness, and the music trends of the moment. It is often described as a "rock 'n' roll Studio 54," except there are no quaaludes in evidence and there isn't exactly a twenty-first-century equivalent of Andy Warhol or Truman Capote on the guest list—even though there are probably a few who would lay claim to that stratosphere. Aside from that, though, there are enough similarities to justify the comparison. Which brings us to the scene at the door.

Like Studio 54 and later clubs of that caliber, Motherfucker is a dictatorship at the door and a democracy on the dance floor. So, once you get past the doorman's discerning eye, you end up dancing among an eclectic gathering that includes celebrities, glam gays, neo new wave girls, goth rock transsexuals, and ambiguously bisexual boys from the boroughs. For the four years that Thomas has been in charge of dictating the club's ropes, he has earned a roster of not-exactly-flattering nicknames. "Door Bitch" is the most famous—and the one that's stuck—but there's also "Door Whore," "Velvet Ropes Nazi," "Glamosaurus Rex," "Buzzkill Bitch," or simply "That Stupid

Queen"—that last one is usually uttered by an underage, Staten Island homophobe who never gets in.

Whenever a camera or a reporter's tape recorder is thrust in Thomas's direction—which is often—he enthusiastically rises to his own defense.

"People think I'm an elitist asshole, but I'm actually not. I don't want to ruin anyone's night," he will say earnestly, again and again. "If you want to get into a club where I'm at the door, you need to think ahead. Pick a look and work it: Bowie, Bauhaus, or Blondie—but not Limp Bizkit." Like Steve Rubell—the manager of Studio 54 who also acted as one of the club's doormen—Thomas believes in creating great parties by "curating" the right mix of people. The job is a dictatorship, nonetheless—and there will always be some pissed-off party-hoppers who won't make the grade and will be sent straight to the nightlife gulag. If only they had invested in that vintage Deborah Harry garbage bag dress instead of a beige Anne Klein suit.

Before the Roxy opens for the night, Thomas and Maura busy themselves with scattering copies of *Paper* and promo CDs around the club. A crew of workers are hanging multicolored balloons and freak show murals around the dance floor and plugging in popcorn and cotton candy machines. The organizers of Motherfucker have chosen a circus theme that not only channels the literal idea of the big top, but also *Circus,* a hard-rock magazine from the 'seventies. As far as New York nightlife is concerned, the circus has always been a reliable theme, from the roller boogie clowns at Studio 54 to the cross-dressed trapeze artists at the darkly decadent Disco 2000—an early 'nineties club that was hosted by Michael Alig, a club kid who was later sent to jail for murdering a drug dealer.

"Okay, everyone," Thomas addresses the gathering of bouncers, assistant door people, and promoters who are standing in a circle near the coat check area. "There's going to be two lines tonight: general admission and will-call will line up against the side of the building and guest list guests will form a parallel line. Max and Phil will be in charge of the guest list, while I'll handle the VIPs. Also press and industry people who need to get in right away." Clearly, Thomas is the ringleader of tonight's door scene circus. Patrick, one of the evening's bouncers, looks slightly bored. Even though the Motherfucker crowd is known to love their cocktails in excess, it's rare that fights break out that would require revelers to be forcefully evicted. This isn't the sort of party that attracts a significant number of déclassé rogues, like the people who flock to scores of other clubs around the city. Still, Patrick will be there to back up Thomas's swift door judgments—in the event that a ruthlessly rejected clubgoer gets out of hand, he'll be there to keep things in line.

Thomas, Max, Phil, and Patrick file out to the front of the club where a pair of workers are installing an arch made from silver foil, letter-shaped balloons that spell out "Motherfucker." The door staff takes their positions around "the box"—the busiest area within the velvet ropes, where guests are admitted, their IDs checked, and their hands stamped before they are hastily shuttled into the venue. Of course, things don't always move as smoothly as the door staff wishes: without fail, there are plenty of people with tall tales of why they don't have their IDs ("It's in my gold lamé jeans, but I decided to change into this chartreuse tube skirt and forgot about it."), the zoned-out girls who wait till the last minute to start rifling through their cluttered handbags in search of their driver's license, and the chatty Cathys who linger around the doorman so they can fill him in on such topics as the eight different products they put in their hair that night.

"That's very nice, darling," Thomas will inform them in a tone that adeptly blends diplomacy with a spritz of impatience, throwing his head back for a burst of stagey laughter when need be. But the gales of laughter can instantly shift to torrential downpours of tongue-lashings if things get chaotic—a high-volume burst of disciplinary vitriol that would make a dominatrix blush.

"I don't want to see ANYONE standing IN FRONT OF THE BARRICADES! If you are not on the list you need to LINE UP AGAINST THE WALL and have your IDs OUT and IN. YOUR. HAND!"

Or, if a venue is nearly full to capacity, Thomas will turn to the waiting crowd and in a booming voice announce, "If you are NOT a regular or you are NOT on the guest list or if I DON'T KNOW YOU, or if I DON'T LIKE YOU then you are NOT GETTING INTO THIS PARTY!"

Often, about five seconds after this doomy proclamation, some frothy little drag queen—some whisper of a geisha—ensconced in nineteen yards of mauve tulle and five layers of delicate white face powder, will float haughtily past the long line over to Thomas, who welcomes her with open arms and a shower of drink tickets. The two hundred people stranded outside, who now have zero hope of the hedonistic evening they've anticipated, will want to surge forward like ravenous ghouls and devour the entrails of the geisha and the doorman in one fell swoop. But they won't dare. They may groan and beg—more than a few will even burst into tears—but they will not jeopardize their chances of getting into the club on their next visit. No one wants to be permanently branded a party pariah by the Door Bitch.

Tonight's rock'n'roll circus is hosted by a club that is large enough to accommodate all who are eligible for admission (i.e., they are at least eighteen years old, are "working a look," or have some kind of inner glamour—like, say, writing for *The New York Post*). As guests begin to arrive and obediently file into one of the two lines, as per Thomas's constant haranguing, gaggles of clowns on stilts begin juggling bowling pins and flaming batons in the street in front of the Roxy. In between juggling bouts, a few bitch-slap each other with their outsized clown-gloved hands. A clown with Marilyn Manson–influenced stage makeup—who seems to have indulged in some "powdering" earlier in the evening—hops back and forth, from one stilt leg to another, in front of Thomas.

THOMAS'S TOP TEN TIPS for GETTING PAST THE ROPES

1. GO WITH STELLA McCARTNEY OR IN STELLA McCARTNEY. If Stella isn't available, Alexander McQueen, Marc Jacobs, or Isaac Mizrahi for Target are acceptable plus ones (or ensemble choices).

2. WORK A LOOK! Don't look like you've just been hit by a Banana Republic delivery truck. Think Carlos D. of Interpol at the opening of the new Dior Homme boutique in Transylvania, *not* Josh Groban at a Celine Dion fragrance launch.

3. DON'T FALL FOR THE *SEX AND THE CITY* FACTOR. Don't get us wrong: We love what stylist Patricia Field has done with raising young women's fashion awareness. However, there is a downside to the SATC phenomenon. It's one thing to look as if you've just stepped off of John Galliano's runway, but it's quite

Continued

"Didyouseemecatchthatflamingbatonwithmy mouth?" he asks Thomas with teeth-grinding excitement. "That's great," Thomas says dryly as he navigates around him to catch the attention of a tall young woman with a black bob haircut who is wearing a circus-influenced couture gown by designer John Galliano. "Darling! You look amazing!" he gushes as he places his body between her and the hyper clown. He kisses both cheeks and places some drink tickets in her black-lace-gloved hand. "*Loved* your story on chinoiserie and celebrity homes," Thomas gushes.

"Thank you!" the woman smiles warmly. "I saw your pals, the Gastineaus, last night at the *Avenue* mag party." Thomas, who also wears the hat of publicist, recently worked on some public relations for the *Gastineau Girls* reality show. "That's quite a fashion competition those two have going on," the woman remarks as she tucks the drink tickets into her Dior handbag.

"Oh, those gals," Thomas says, as his eyes begin to look past the woman's ruffled shoulder, making sure there are no flaming batons careening toward her. "I'm just glad my mother doesn't compete with me like that. She just wouldn't look right working a Vivienne Westwood cummerbund and face glitter." Thomas

[14]

lifts the rope for her and she sweeps through, gliding past the bouncers. A young man sporting a Lords of the New Church T-shirt and a Robert Smith hairdo seems transfixed by the fishtail hem of the woman's gown as it disappears into the darkness of the club. Thomas surveys the crowd of people who are waiting in front of the ropes. The two lines stretch past the length of the club and around the corner where Eighteenth Street meets the West Side Highway. The gathering resembles a casting call for a Tim Burton remake of *Vampire Circus*—acid rock clowns, transsexual lion tamers, sadomasochistic Siegfrieds and Roys, KISS doppelgangers, rockabilly cat girls, shirtless lean boys in black leather pants with ringleader top hats, kabuki white-faced dominatrices, metallic, silver-faced Pierrots, lipsticked and bewigged male Satanists, Chucky the killer clown, Bowie-meets-Bozos, Ozzy Osbournes on a Barnum and Bailey bender. Even a few blasé boys in Led Zeppelin and Iron Maiden T-shirts have taken the time to lipstick red clown mouths on and around their lips. The clowns in the street have graduated from flaming baton juggling to full-on fire breathing. A cliché of New York nightlife—"Fellini-esque"—applies.

another to look like you've mugged a transvestite hooker for her outfit. If your skirt is too short, you're wearing animal prints that don't match, or you're wearing heels that you can't walk in, there's a good chance the door bitch will feed you alive to Joan Rivers.

4. ALWAYS HAVE YOUR ID READY, PLEASE. This will enable the expedient flow of traffic and make the doorman's job easier. Acceptable forms of ID include: driver's license, passport, or birth certificate. Unacceptable forms of ID include: fake ID bought in the Republic of Congo, the before and after photos from your recent nip-tuck, or your mom. (This actually happened once—a boyish clubber of dubious age brought his mother along to vouch for him.)

5. BE POLITE AND OBEDIENT. Try this: Walk up to the doorman—who is almost always busy—and apologize for interrupting him. Apologize for breathing his air. Apologize again for your very existence. Follow his

Continued

instructions closely. If the doorman says "If you're on the list, go stand in line #4" or "If you're not on the list, please fill out these forms in triplicate" or "Pop quiz! Please recite the lyrics to LCD Soundsystem's 'Losing My Edge'," it will be in your best interest to comply.

6. KNOW THE NAME OR TITLE OF THE GUEST LIST YOU ARE ON. This way, you won't be confused with the Brooks Brothers suit–wearing broker standing behind you. How do hopeful clubbers get on a guest list in the first place, you might ask? One way is through a night club's Web site. Another is to attend a party and ask the doorman if you can meet the promoter. If all else fails, try writing a letter to your local senator, your rabbi, or Michael Moore.

7. TRY A LITTLE CHARM. A compliment never hurt anybody, and the doorman usually has an ego that needs constant stroking. Try: "You look really young and thin . . . tonight!" or "Your hair smells terrific!" or

Continued

"HAVE YOUR IDs OUT AND HAVE THEM IN YOUR HANDS!" Thomas thunders again and again. A girl in a sequined trapeze artist leotard covered with rock band buttons—the Yeah Yeah Yeahs, Blondie, Berlin—opens her purse, but pulls out a compact mirror instead of her ID. Thomas shoots her a disapproving glare. Suddenly, the sea of clowns in the street parts for a long limousine that is pulling up to the front of the club. The door opens and a thin, androgynous man clad in a white Yves Saint Laurent-like woman's suit and flowing white silk scarf emerges. Mirrored sunglasses, Rocky Horror red lips, the hauteur of a young Faye Dunaway . . . every head in the long line turns in this thin, white duke's direction and all conversation is put on pause. Michael T., the reigning DJ and founder of Motherfucker, has arrived. Thomas is already holding the ropes open to ensure Michael's diva march from limo door to club door maintains its fashion runway smoothness. Michael gives Thomas a quick air kiss, ignoring a few shouts of "Michael T.!" that erupt from the crowd.

"I'M NOT SEEING ENOUGH IDs OUT AND IN PEOPLE'S HANDS!!" Thomas snarls, snapping the crowd out of their brief glam trance. Tonight has a dual system for entry—eighteen-to-twenty-year-olds receive a red stamp on their hands, which means "no alcohol," and twenty-one and over get the green stamp, which allows them to buy drinks—and there is a high surveillance agent in charge of filtering out those who show up with fake IDs. That agent, Derek Neen, is a bit of a New York club legend and has been a doorman in the city since 1989.

"You can smell the mendacity in the air on a night like this," Derek says slyly, paraphrasing Big Daddy in Tennessee Williams' *Cat on a Hot Tin Roof.* Judging from the glee that Derek sometimes derives from toying with people at the ropes, a more apt sentiment might be the notorious line from *Apocalypse Now*: "I love the smell of napalm in the morning." Thomas's senior by more than a decade, Derek is a seasoned doorman, albeit a low-profile one.

A girl who seems to have imagined herself to be Siouxsie Sioux as a Weimar Republic–era circus performer makes it past the ropes but is pulled over by Patrick the bouncer and handed over to Derek for ID interrogation. Seems the punkette princess has arrived with no ID. "But I'm twenty-three," she pleads, her red-glittered top lip quivering slightly. Derek looks her up and

"Oh my god, your new tan looks so natural!"

8. STRATEGIC NAME-DROPPING. If you're going to resort to name-dropping, know the right names to drop. Names that tend to work are club owners, club promoters or the head of security. Names that do not work are the club janitor's drug dealer, the bartender's manicurist, or Paris Hilton (*everyone* thinks they're friends with Paris).

9. BE PREPARED TO WAIT. Patience is a virtue and good things come to those who wait. Due to space limitations, there's always a chance that the doorman will ask you to wait for thirty minutes or more. We suggest you come prepared to amuse yourself. Chat with your friends about which "over-the-counter" medication you took before you went out that night, call your mother from your cell phone just to say "I love you," or bring the *New York Times* crossword puzzle.

Continued

10. TRY ASKING "MAY I COME IN?"
Many people are too busy deviously thinking of ways to get past the doorman—lying, bribing, threatening, pulling together a look from a nearby garbage can—but don't realize that the easiest way to get past the ropes is simply to ask. You may be pleasantly surprised by the doorman's reaction (or you may flee in terror with your tail between your legs).

down and then fixes his cool gaze on her now-moist eyes. "When is your birthday?"

"July tw . . . elfth . . . nineteen seventy-nine," she says, stuttering slightly.

"Well, that doesn't add up," Derek says. "Try again, sweetheart." She adjusts the date, then her age, then makes a last-ditch effort by citing her high school graduation year. Derek frowns. She gets the red stamp.

Meanwhile, Thomas has his own headache to deal with. Two Latino boy/girl couples, who have waited patiently in the general admission line for over thirty minutes, have been denied entry. The guys are slim and dressed in white T-shirts and olive drab army fatigues, and they resemble Nicaraguan guerrillas apart from the fact that one of them has his hair in pigtails. The girls are wearing short skirts and mildly flirty blouses—very Jennifer Lopez lite. "I'm sorry, but there's a dress code tonight," Phil informs them calmly and asks them to step aside. They make a second appeal to Thomas, who brushes them off with a curt "Sorry, my door team has made their decision. Please step away from the ropes."

"This is discrimination!" one of the men howls angrily. "What's wrong with the way I'm dressed?!" He lingers by the ropes and begins surveying the clubgoers who have passed muster. A group of late-forty-something, potbellied drag queens wearing tatty sequined polyester dresses, who look like they've been exhumed from the original production of *La Cage Aux Folles,* are waddling toward the entrance of the club. The door staff doesn't bother to ask them for their IDs. "Look at her!" one of the Latinos yells angrily while pointing at the portliest of the queens. "I'm much better looking than her!" Patrick tells him they need to take their cause up with Thomas. "That bitch won't give us the time of day!" he screams, gesturing at Thomas, who has coolly turned his back on the whole scene. Patrick walks over to Thomas to verify the decision and returns. "The doorman has cited 'dress code.' I'm sorry, you can't come in," he tells the couples. They eventually give up and leave.

Thomas's decision to back up Phil's call is controversial. "I think Thomas was intimidated by their urban Latino vibe," Patrick says discreetly to Derek.

Derek nods. "They seemed like they were right on the edge of getting rock 'n' roll freaky . . . like, they would have had a few drinks and the boys might have taken their shirts off and all of them would have had a good time. I would have let them in."

"Yeah, but sometimes it's hard to judge the crowd and how some people will act once they get inside," Patrick adds diplomatically.

As the crowd swells outside the ropes and more and more cabs begin pulling up to the club, the number of people being turned away is well into the double digits. Loitering in front of the barricades, away from the ropes, this carnival of lost club souls ponders their options: Try again and hope the doorman has a change of heart? Try another club? Go back to Staten Island for a change of clothing?

One such group—three Italian-American men—who are donned in untucked button-down shirts and unremarkable jeans, and whose hair is drenched in the requisite amount of Gotti-strength hair gel, stand a few feet behind Thomas, clinging to a few shreds of their dignity. The Guidos, the scourge of any hip club, have made their predictable appearance. No club with even the slightest edge of cool wants them, and there is an almost unacknowledged racism in the ceremonious shutting-out of the Guido. Thomas—who happens to be an Italian-American from New Jersey—knows how to deal with the Guidos who dare to defy his door decree.

"Honey, I'm from New Jersey, okay? And even I'm cooler than you," he will say with a calculated air of self-deprecation and cartoonish arrogance. Such put-downs occasionally reap rewards: there have been more than a few Guidos who have returned to subsequent parties in ripped, nipple-exposing, Alien Sex Fiend T-shirts, cascades of glitter clinging to their arms, faces, and Gotti dos. At a recent Motherfucker, one Guido made a reappearance with his industrial-strength gelled hair dyed orange, a safety pin in his ear, and a shredded and paint-splattered "Kiss Me, I'm Italian" T-shirt. Thomas dubbed him "Gianni Rotten."

But tonight, the trio of Guidos outside the Roxy possesses no glitter and no chutzpah; their working-class assertiveness momentarily caught in a deer-in-the-headlights haze. They stand silently outside the club, gazing longingly at a pair of reed-thin drag queens in Pucci sheaths, who are arm in arm with a muscular young man who is sporting a red clown nose and wearing a shirt made entirely from safety pins. Thomas turns around and notices the gawking Guidos and lets out a growl that causes all three of them to jump in startled unison. "EXCUSE ME. You CAN'T stand there, you need to MOVE along!" They move closer to the barricade and make a meek appeal to Patrick, who tells them there's nothing he can do.

When they return to their position on the sidewalk, Thomas begins spitting nails. "You need to MOVE ALONG and if that's too much of an effort for you, I can have the bouncers PUUUSH YOU DOWN THE STREET!" He makes a sweeping motion with both arms as he pronounces "puuush," as if casting a banishing spell. The Guidos hang their heads and saunter away slowly, leaving behind the perplexing visions of a world that is rarely experienced beyond the confines of their TV sets.

At around three A.M., the crowd outside has dwindled to a few beefy boys in David Barton Gym T-shirts, who have wandered over from a nearby weekly gay event. Even though there is nothing vaguely circus or rock 'n' roll about them, Thomas charitably lifts the ropes and welcomes them in. "Have a good time, boys," he says before turning to Patrick. "Okay, I'm going inside now, I think my job is done. If Courtney Love escapes from Bellevue or wherever she's holed up now and decides to show up, give me a holler. I'll try to rustle up some drink tickets for her."

Despite his exhaustion, Thomas sprints up the carpeted steps of the Roxy, which are littered with burst balloons, squashed popcorn bags, feathers, sequins, and trampled, unopened condom packages that were given out by an AIDS prevention group. When he enters the main ballroom, a performance has just started on the main stage. The heavy metal circus midgets who had been gyrating atop the bar for hours are now sitting in pools of spilled cocktails, happily enjoying the show. On stage, a large group of drag queens—led by a performer named Peppermint Gummybear—are reenacting scenes from the 1980 film *Fame.* A chorus line of queens bedecked in leotards, tiny spandex shorts, and leg warmers are lined up for a mock theater tryout. "You want fame?" Peppermint shouts at them. "Well, fame *costs.* And right here is where you start paying. With sweat."

The crowd—who now have more than a few cocktails under their Alexander McQueen belts—erupt in ecstatic cheers. The onstage queens begin dancing and leaping to the *Fame* theme song. As Thomas is laughing at Peppermint's Debbie Allen send-up, a young man in a Rancid T-shirt slides up next to him, slips something in his pocket, and kisses him on the cheek. "Thanks for another great party," he grins, and then disappears into the crowd. Thomas reaches in his pocket and finds a joint. He smiles and plunges into the crowd on the dance floor where more than a few people grab him, kiss him, yell out his name. A person of indeterminate gender, who is wearing tight red patent leather pants, a matching jacket, and a striped red-and-black top hat, grabs Thomas's ass as he moves through the crowd. "Hey, sweetie" Thomas says, perhaps a little too wearily. Very New York Dolls, Thomas thinks to himself, smug in his knowledge of rock 'n' roll's more ephemeral fashion statements. More people sidle up to him to say hi and he wonders—as he does on many nights—if he is really among friends or just fickle party people who rely on him to skirt the long lines and admission fees of the clubs he works. He tries not to dwell on that for now, as he pushes his way past the made-up masses, toward the DJ booth, the nerve center of Motherfucker.

Looming over the control panel, like a shining, white Valkyrie who has hijacked the Starship *Enterprise,* is Michael T. "Hey baby," he says, looking up for a second before returning to some lever-and-knob adjusting. "How did the door go?"

"Great. It's an amazing crowd. I had to do very little editing at the door," Thomas says as he surveys the revelers on the dance floor who number close to one thousand. Like most tastemakers working in New York—designers, fashion stylists, publicists—he relishes the use of the word "editing." In fact, many discerning urbanites fancy themselves the offspring of Diana Vreeland, the legendary *Vogue* magazine editor who turned the art of "editing"—separating the wheat from chaff, as they say—into a sort of style Darwinism. "The fags, freaks, and fashionistas are out in full force tonight," Thomas declares grandly.

"You can say that again," Michael says, as if he is only half listening, checking his lipstick in a small hand mirror. "And people thought downtown was dead."

"The cynics have been decreeing that downtown has died since I was in the fifth grade," Thomas jokes. "Or was it just Michael Musto who was doing the decreeing?" he adds, referring to the longtime columnist for *The Village Voice.* "That is, until he pronounced Motherfucker 'the party of the millennium.'"

"Thanks for that commercial break, dear," Michael says with rehearsed bitchiness. "Chips on my Shoulder" by 'eighties band Soft Cell starts booming through the club's sound system as the *Fame* imitators are leaving the stage. Thomas watches a group of kids who are wearing disturbing doll masks spastically bob up and down. He pulls out his cell phone and scrolls to the number of his car service.

A few minutes later, Thomas is collapsed in the back of a Lincoln Town Car, counting the money that Johnny T., one of the organizers of the party, has paid him for his night's work. Emotionally and physically exhausted, the people and events from the night's proceedings are still swimming in his head. All the kids and the looks—was New York like this five years ago? He knows it was like this twenty years ago . . . he's heard many stories and collected the old magazines documenting the scene: *Details, Interview, Project X.* He wonders if he has helped shape the revitalization of the club scene. *Am I being grandiose in thinking that?* he wonders. And how long will it last? There are some nights when he goes home feeling unhappy, lonely, un-fulfilled . . . like an unmarried, clipboard-wielding casting agent overseeing a cattle call of desperate, lackluster ingénues. But not tonight. Tonight was nothing short of a triumph for New York nightlife. Or, as close as one can get these days . . .

Thomas enters the tiny apartment he shares with a fashion writer named Anya. Strewn about the kitchen and mini living room are his roommate's sequined dresses, elaborate hats, and polka-dot print pumps. "This place looks like a new wave flop-house," Thomas says out loud into the semidarkness. He stum-bles into his tiny, cluttered bedroom, knocking over a towering pile of magazines, which crash into another tower comprised of stacked videos—a mix of porn, promo music videos, and a few obscure 'eighties films—sending the tapes toppling to the floor. Thomas merely sighs, clears a path through the debris, and collapses onto a pile of dirty clothes that camouflage a nar-row mattress that lies frameless on the floor. As the first rays of the morning sun peak through the disheveled blinds, the Door Bitch is out cold.

2 .

Give me some shit, you can give me the cribs
You can give me whatever, just pass the Courvoisier.
—BUSTA RHYMES AND DIDDY

Eight A.M. is far too early for New York's top club doorman to be getting out of bed. Despite being New York's "door god" (he has ripped the recent press clip from a nightlife rag proclaiming him as such and taped it to a nearby mirror), Thomas, like everyone else in the city, has to deal with the reality of life in New York—which means holding down several jobs in order to pay the rent. Today it's working backstage at the 7th on Sixth fashion shows in Bryant Park. The first show is a young L.A. designer named Jared Gold, which he knows will be a snap. It's the second show, Baby Phat, the hip-hop label lorded over by Kimora Lee Simmons, wife of music mega-mogul Russell Simmons, that he knows is going to take every ounce of his guard-dog muscle. Kimora is known in the press for her famous threat, "I will beat a bitch's ass!" her marijuana and careless driving bust (the police mug shot is a camp classic in gossip circles), and her legions of celebrity and thug admirers. Thomas shivers at the thought of it.

The previous night he'd been up until three A.M. at the office of MAO PR, the fashion public relations company producing the Baby Phat show, making callbacks for seating assignments. MAO's office had been besieged with calls from every Snoop Doggy Dogg wannabe and DJ so-and-so who wanted to attend Kimora's show with their respective posses, despite the fact that each invitation admits one person and one person only. Thomas nervously envisions fifty tons of bling-bling and fur crashing through the front doors of the tent, but consoles himself that there will be security—after all, 7th on Sixth executive director Fern Mallis maintains order at her shows with an iron fist.

After some mental pep talking, Thomas is ready to face down droves of jaded editors, narcissistic celebrities, and gangsta label whores. On the subway ride to Bryant Park he leafs through the latest issue of *US Weekly*, pausing at a photo of Kimora on the red carpet at the Tony Awards. She's wearing a red dress with white polka dots that is so cleavage-revealing, the fabric resembles two narrow Band-Aids running down the sides of her torso. Looking at the photo, Thomas gets a sick feeling deep in the pit of his stomach. *My god, this Baby Phat show is going to be so scary,* he thinks to himself as the car doors open at the Forty-second Street stop.

Jared Gold's show, which starts promptly at noon, goes smoothly. Gold, known for his fashionable homage to the Black Dahlia murder case, showed humble yet colorful frocks on a runway decorated with a Warholesque silver balloon décor theme. Thomas knew this was the calm before the storm. At a pre-Baby Phat meeting in the park outside the tents Thomas meets Bubbles, the Simmons's celebrity wrangler. Thomas looks her up and down coolly, as he does almost every night with the people who gather hopefully outside the ropes of the clubs he works at. Bubbles is wearing a baby blue Juicy Couture track suit and enormous Dior sunglasses. Her hair is slightly unkempt. This *woman in the ghetto track suit, with that ratty, natty hair, does this job?* Thomas thinks to himself incredulously as he shakes her hand. *Are they kidding? They let her talk to celebrities?* He notices Bubbles's eyes zeroing in on his heavily glossed lips and then move up a few inches to his shellacked bangs. Her top lip twitches slightly and he knows he's being judged as well.

As more people from Kimora's office show up for the meeting, Thomas realizes he is out of his element. This is not the aloof rocker crowd he is used to dealing with, the crowd that shares his lifestyle. He's nervous, intimidated, but tries to hide it. During the meeting, Bubbles rattles off a list of the celebrities expected to attend. She sounds like she's auditioning for a correspondent job on the E! channel.

After the meeting, Thomas makes his way over to the backstage entrance of Baby Phat with a radio headset, a handful of backstage passes, and a clipboard full of the names of approved press, celebrities, and friends. He positions himself behind the check-in table, where a blonde intern from FIT has been waiting patiently. Several security guards stand watch by the backstage entrance. As Thomas applies another layer of lip gloss, he surveys the list. CNN, NBC, *Good Morning America, Fashion File,* photographers from *People, US, Vogue* . . . these are all heavy hitters, he thinks. In the tent next door, Kimora's husband Russell is presenting his show for his own line, Phat Farm. Thomas can hear the muffled thump-thump of a mash-up that has combined Blondie's "Rapture" with an overtly aggressive Tupac Shakur song. The sampled sound of gunshots punctuate the track. The sick feeling returns to the pit of Thomas's stomach.

Suddenly, Kimora sweeps into the backstage waiting area with an entourage of eight people. Thomas recognizes them from previous meetings: Kimora's assistant, Russell's assistant, her business manager, the president of Baby Phat, and a few friends. Towering over six feet tall, the half-Japanese, half-black diva is dressed in an emerald green blazer, jeans, and stiletto heels. *Glossy* lips. She rushes past Thomas into the backstage area, barely acknowledging him, hair and hoop earrings swooshing past his nose. *She's beautiful,* Thomas thinks to himself. He peers into the backstage area where stylists and dressers are busy tending to the clothes. Thomas can't help noticing that Kimora seems lost; she doesn't look like a designer entering the backstage of her own collection, but more like a celebrity being hustled backstage to do press. After doing a few interviews, she leaves and goes next door to be with Russell at the Phat Farm show.

People start arriving in the backstage foyer, peering over the top of Thomas's clipboard. They aren't exactly nobodies: A reporter from *TV Guide,* an editor from *The Fader,* a photographer from Ron Galella's studio. However, none of them are on the list. They are followed by legit guests—reporters from *Vibe,* Patrick McMullan, Juicy Couture–clad friends of the Simmonses. Within minutes Thomas is down to five backstage passes, with dozens of guests still expected to arrive. "I need more passes; it's getting really crazy back here," Thomas radios to Brian, MAO's PR director, who is working the front of the house where invited guests are being checked in. For a few moments there is no response, but through his headset Thomas can hear the loud murmur of a crowd, followed by the sound of breaking glass, some shouts, and then the sound of glass being crushed underfoot. Finally Brian responds from his headset.

"Thomas, it's a goddamn zoo up here! All of the people who didn't get into Phat Farm, plus like four dozen DJs, each with their ten uninvited friends are crammed into the lobby in front of our check-in table, trying to crash Baby Phat. And now everyone is getting drunk at the open Courvoisier bar and there's broken glass everywhere! What genius decided to serve free liquor in real glasses during back-to-back hip-hop shows?!"

"Jesus! Listen, Brian, I'm running out of backstage passes. Do you have any more?"

"Yes, we have another stash. We didn't want to give you all

of them at once because we knew Kimora's people would shake you down for them before the important press people arrived. I'll send a runner back there with more."

"Thanks, Brian." As Thomas is saying these words he looks up toward the entrance of the Phat Farm backstage. The show has finished and people are streaming out. Between the Phat Farm and Baby Phat backstage foyers, 7th on Sixth has erected a barricade of ropes and stanchions, and, ideally, the backstage guests are to file out of the tent on one side of the barrier, exiting to the outside. Unfortunately, the rowdy hip-hop crowd has other plans in mind. *Oh my lord, what are they doing?* Thomas is thinking. He watches in horror as throngs of Phat Farm fans decked out in gold jewelry, oversized shirts and jackets, and real and faux Fendi, Chanel, and Dior begin walking under, over, and around the barricade with impunity, before pushing the whole setup aside altogether. They begin waving their Phat Farm backstage passes in front of Thomas, assuming they will get them into Baby Phat.

Thomas launches into one of his authoritative, crowd-control speeches, similar to the ones he recites night after night to would-be clubgoers. "If you are not on this guest list and do not have a backstage pass to get into Baby Phat, you can't come in through this backstage entrance. You have to go arooooound," he gestures didactically with a long, circular motion, "to the front of the tent." He is greeted with blank stares. The crowd edges up closer. Members of the crowd move toward the security guards and hold their passes up higher. "That won't get you into this backstage," one of the security guards tells the crowd repeatedly. "But I'm friends with Kimora," a girl wearing a pink Juicy Couture tracksuit and outsized Chanel sunglasses says to him haughtily. "I don't care if you're friends with Mayor Bloomberg and George W., you ain't gettin' into this backstage," the guard barks at her.

The small room is now packed with gatecrashers, about thirteen people deep all the way back to the door. No one makes a move to leave—this is a crowd that won't take no for an answer. Suddenly, without warning, a section of the crowd comes careening toward the check-in table, violently pinning Thomas and the blonde intern against the wall. "What the hell . . . ?" Thomas looks up and sees Kimora, Russell, and a giant posse of handlers whipping through the crowd toward the backstage. A few people in the crowd yell out to them. "Yo, Russell, whattup?!" A tall man in a Nelly T-shirt and a girl half his size quickly slide into the posse's wake, only to be thwarted by a security guard before they reach the door.

As Thomas is pushing the table forward a few inches and trying to regain his bearings, Kimora's assistant, a stocky man in his late twenties, in a baggy flannel shirt, baggy khakis, and a Phat Farm baseball cap, pops out through the backstage door. "Uhm, excuse me, I need more passes so I can get some of Kimora's friends in." *This is just crazy, CNN and NBC haven't arrived yet and this baggy number wants to shuttle in another dozen* *members of the Juicy Couture squad,* Thomas thinks. *Doesn't he understand the importance of the press?* He radios Brian again. "*Where* is the runner with those passes?!*"

"She's on her way Thomas, but we've got a, uhm, situation developing up here." Brian sounds panicked. Thomas hears the crunching of broken glass again.

"Don't tell me people are fighting with broken Courvoisier bottles," Thomas says worriedly.

"Not yet, but the fire marshal and the police are on their way, and we're not even sure there's going to be a show. Things are so out of hand, we have thirty security guards up here with us. And they've *locked* the front doors so no one else can get in. The doors are fucking *locked!* So, we have about three hundred drunk hip-hoppers jammed in here who are *not* on the list, and nary a *Vogue* editor or Bloomingdales buyer in sight. I don't even want to *think* about Kal Ruttenstein trying to navigate this mess."

Thomas shudders at the thought of the overweight, ailing Bloomingdales honcho taking a spill through a stretch of broken glass. "The doors are locked?! That doesn't sound good."

"And you should see the circus going on outside on the steps. Jennifer Saunders and Joanna Lumley are filming an episode of *Ab Fab.* More Baby Phat fans are getting out of limos, and I'm sure *none* of them are on the list. Bill Cunningham is running up and down the stairs taking pictures."

"Of course he is," Thomas say dryly. "I smell a tracksuit theme in the next *New York Times* Styles section." Thomas then looks up and sees several policemen walking out of the Phat

Farm backstage. *Jesus Christ,* he thinks, *this would* never *happen at an Oscar de la Renta show.* The most drama that happens there is when Amy Fine Collins or Pat Buckley orders a stray fashion assistant out of their seat. The policemen push their way through the crowd and enter the Baby Phat backstage. Thomas's headset crackles to life again. It's the head of MAO PR. "Thomas, this is Mauricio. ARE YOU THERE?" *Oh god, this has to be so bad.* Thomas breaks into a sweat. "I'm here Mauricio, what's wrong?"

"Listen, we can't get people through the front of the tent anymore, so I'm sending them around back to you. I have two editors here from *Women's Wear Daily,* Brooke and Agnes, and they *have* to get in."

This is like secret agent nonsense, Thomas is thinking. "Mauricio, I don't know how I can get people in here . . . I can't even get people from the door to me because of the crowd!"

"Thomas, you *have* to get them in. Just do whatever you have to do."

Thomas goes through the logistics in his head. Security has to get them through the crowd and into the backstage entrance. They need backstage passes or they'll be in violation of the fire code. They have to walk through hordes of Simmons hangers-on, dressers and models, out onto the runway and over to their seats. *Can't we just send them home and messenger a copy of the video to them tomorrow?* Thomas wonders. Suddenly, across the room Thomas spots the *WWD* editors. One is wearing a Prada trench coat and the other has on what looks to be a vintage shrug. They have annoyed "we're *just* trying to do our jobs, why must things be *so* difficult" grimaces on their faces, a common facial expression during fashion week. The tent could be on fire or a model could be ODing on the runway and their attitude would still be "can I just take my gift bag, go back to the office, and file my copy now, please?" As security is escorting the editors through the crowd, an intern appears from backstage with more passes. "The fire department is up front now," she tells Thomas. "And there's a whole crew of VIPs stranded on the front steps. Mauricio is sending them around to you now."

"I hope Bubbles is taking good care of them." Thomas is imagining her arm in arm with Lil' Kim, walking back and forth in front of Bill Cunningham's camera.

"Bubbles? She went to the store to buy some Juicy Fruit gum and never came back," the intern informs him.

That figures, thinks Thomas. He looks down at his list. Still no *Fashion File* or CNN. He fantasizes about a bulldozer scooping up the crowd of crashers ala *Soylent Green* to make room for the TV cameras. Just then Thomas spots two attractive black women—one slender, one plump—on the other side of the room, eyeing the crowd and stepping back outside. He starts shouting to the security guards. "Oh my god, Vanessa Williams and Jennifer Holiday are on the other side of the room, you have to go help them get over here!" Three guards make a move, pushing the crowd to the sides and forming a narrow tunnel leading from the outside door to Thomas.

Vanessa and Jennifer are ushered through and within seconds they are followed by a conga line of VIPs: Queen Latifah, Al Sharpton and his wife, Andre Leon Talley (sans Anna Wintour) from *Vogue,* Mary J. Blige, Patricia Field, Tyra Banks, Mya and Wyclef Jean. Shouts and catcalls erupt from the crowd. The security guards move back toward Thomas and the crowd fills in the tunnel behind them. "Wait!" Thomas screams. "You left Brittany Murphy back there!"

The guards muscle their way back through the crowd toward the blonde actress who has linked arms with a black woman with cropped hair wearing a Chanel tweed jacket and lots of African jewelry. When they get to Thomas, he recognizes her as former *New York Times* fashion writer Constance White. "Hi! I'm here to interview Brittany!" Thomas looks at her skeptically. "Constance, we don't have you scheduled to do any interviews until *after* the show." Constance fingers the ivory beads that are wrapped around her throat and tightens her grip around Brittany's arm. "But I want to do it now," she says with a calm air of media authority. Without taking his eyes off her, Thomas talks into his headset. "Brian, it's Thomas. Constance is telling me she wants to interview Brittany now. Who authorized this?"

"No one did. Tell her she's interviewing everyone after the show." Just as Thomas is about to deliver the news, Kimora's assistant appears again from backstage, grabs Brittany and Constance and drags them inside. "Excuse me, what exactly is it that you do again?" Thomas asks while throwing him a dagger look. "I'm Kimora and Russell's assistant," he replies testily. "I take care of them." He then grabs five more people from the crowd and pulls them backstage with him. "This is ridiculous," Thomas murmurs, and then he says to the security guards "We can't let anyone in unless they have a backstage pass!"

"But Russell was asking to get those people in right now," a guard tells him distractedly as he studies the cleavage of a young Latina woman who is standing conspicuously close to him. Before Thomas can respond, his gaze falls across the room to a brown-haired girl in a jean jacket with a fur collar and an older woman with full lips in a tank top. Thomas recognizes the younger woman and starts yelling at the security guard. "Oh my god, that's Nicky Hilton over there! You have to get her over here RIGHT NOW!" Thomas looks across the room—it seems even more crowded than it was ten minutes ago. What are all these people thinking? They're never going to get in and they shouldn't even be here in the first place. Thomas watches as the head of security and two other guards push their way over to Nicky and her friend. Suddenly he sees them lift Nicky up above the crowd.

Oh Christ, what *are they doing?* Thomas panics. *They're manhandling a Hilton sister!* Before he can say anything, the guards are crowd-surfing Nicky over the heads of the hip-hop mob. "Wooooo! NIC-KEEEY!" a few people holler. The guards and various crowd members surf Nicky toward Thomas, who reaches up and grabs her. She falls into Thomas's arms and gives him a big hug and a non-air kiss. "Hey you!" she squeals as he puts her down and, unfazed, moves toward the backstage like this is just another drive-by party kiss. Next, Nicky's friend is lifted across the crowd in the same manner and the guards literally hand her to Thomas. Oh my god, it's Jade Barrymore, Thomas says to himself. Without a word, Jade casually follows Nicky and the pair head backstage. Thomas peeks in behind them and watches as Russell hands them glasses of champagne. Brian's voice comes through Thomas's headset. "Did you get Nicky and Jade?"

"I sure did. They are already partying with Russell as we speak."

"Good, good. Now see what you can do with the CNN team. They just left the front of the tent about five minutes ago. But make sure they get passes. The fire department made their way through the front and I think they're backstage now."

Thomas looks up and there on the other side of the room is a cameraman and a reporter. The reporter is clutching a microphone as he nervously surveys the crowd. "Okay, guys," Thomas turns to the head of security. "That's the CNN crew. They have to get in here right now and do an interview with Kimora before the show starts." The guards move to the far side of the room. One lifts up the cameraman, another grabs the camera, and surfs them separately over the crowd. Bringing up the rear is the reporter. When the guards drop them in front of Thomas they seem considerably shaken, compared to the nonchalant Nicky and Jade (who are probably on their third round of champagne by now). "I guess this ain't no walk in the park, like covering wars in the Middle East," one of the guards ribs the reporters. "Shit," Thomas says out loud and then radios Brian. "I don't have any more backstage passes and I have the CNN crew standing in front of me."

"Tell the intern to go backstage and grab some passes off the hair and makeup team. No one is going to arrest a hairdresser without a pass while he's blowing out Devon's hair, for crissake."

As Thomas is giving the intern instructions, he feels someone tugging on the sleeve of his J. Lindeberg dress shirt. He turns and a girl in a nylon Adidas tracksuit and big hoop earrings is standing in front of him. "Hey, I'm DJ Momo." Thomas looks at her blankly. "Don't you know who I am?" she continues. "I sang on the new Heavy D record and I'm supposed to be backstage with Russell and Kimora." *Sure you are honey,* Thomas thinks, and before he can respond, someone is now tapping him on the shoulder. He looks to his left and two girls dressed in asymmetrical skirts, one leopard, one lotus flower print, and matching black tank tops are standing there like the ghost twins in *The Shining.* "Hi! We're in the new girl group City High and we're supposed to be in there right now," one says confidently. "Look! We're even dressed in all Baby Phat!" the other squeaks.

"I don't care if you're wearing the shroud of Turin and Queen Nefertiti's vintage caftan, you're not on my list and you're not getting in." The baggy assistant, now clutching a handful of passes, appears from backstage again, runs into the crowd, grabs two more people, and heads back toward the door.

This is the last straw. Thomas grabs the assistant by the neck before he can reach the door. "Listen. I have a CNN crew standing right here in front of me and *Full Frontal Fashion* and *Fashion File* are on their way. They are all scheduled to interview Kimora and Russell, NOW. Are you going to go inside and tell Kimora that the CNN crew can't come in because you need to pull in more friends?" Thomas tightens his grip around baggy's neck. "Are you going to tell her that the CNN interview is NOT GOING TO HAPPEN because of you? Are you going to be responsible for telling her that RIGHT NOW?" The man just looks at him. *He's going to punch me,* Thomas is thinking.

Thomas lets go of his neck. Stunned, baggy doesn't say a word, but turns around and walks back inside. Just then security delivers the host of *Full Frontal Fashion,* Christina Ha, and her crew. As if by magic, the runner appears from backstage with more passes. "I had to fight over these with one of Kimora's handlers," she tells Thomas, exasperated. Thomas quickly hands the passes to all the crews, pushes them through the backstage entrance, and then turns to the crowd. Looking like a glam rock Moses about to hurl down the Ten Commandments at the disobedient multitude of heathens, he screams "Okay people! In all probability, you are NOT going to get in.

Backstage is full to capacity and the front doors to the tent are closed. GO HOME." The crowd ignores him and moves closer, like hip-hop zombies. Thomas radios Brian. "Brian, it's Thomas. What is happening? Is the show still going to happen?" Brian's radio crackles back, and all Thomas can hear are shouts, broken glass, and then . . . *bloodcurdling screams.* Thomas panics, radioing Mauricio. "Mauricio, can you hear me? What the hell is going on up there?!" Dead silence. The head of security turns to Thomas, "I just spoke with security up front. The show is starting right now." The security guards pull both doors to backstage shut. The bloodcurdling screams are running through Thomas's head, over and over. *Maybe I should go up there and see what happened,* he thinks, *maybe I should call the police. Oh wait,* he thinks, *the police are already* here. *What is going on up there?!* As Thomas frantically goes over every possible gruesome scenario in his head, his thoughts are interrupted by a tall black man in a Sean John suit standing in front of him. "Excuse me, I'm DJ Momo's manager, and my client really needs to be in there right now." DJ Momo is standing beside him with an expression that is half hopeful, half smug.

"You're kidding, right?" Thomas tells him. "Do you have an idea how long these shows last? Even if I could get you in, by the time you got to the runway, Kimora will have already taken her bow and have moved on to threatening to beat at least nine bitch's asses because they looked at Russell the wrong way." DJ Momo crosses her arms, her manager takes out his cell phone. The head of security turns to Thomas again.

"Show's over, dude." As soon as he says these words, the double doors burst open and members of the MAO team come spilling out. Brian and his assistant Autumn are as white as sheets and speechless. "Are you guys okay?!" Thomas asks. The pair slams their clipboards down on the table and Autumn grabs a nearby chair, sits down with her head between her legs, and begins dry-heaving. Thomas looks over at Brian who is also now seated. "What happened??" he asks. Brian bursts into tears. After a few minutes of dry-heaving and crying, Brian is finally able to speak.

"We were nearly trampled up there, it was a stampede! The crowd completely lost control when they were told no one was getting in," Brian says as he begins to compose himself.

"Tell him about the guns, Brian." Autumn says meekly.

"Guns?" Thomas asks incredulously.

"There was a group of guys in front of the check-in table and they wouldn't leave, even after I told them numerous times they were not on the list," Brian explains, his voice shaking. "And three of them flashed open their coats and they were wearing guns in holsters underneath!" Autumn begins dry-heaving again. When she's finished, she looks up at Thomas. "Thomas, that was the *worst* door I've ever done. It was even worse than the night we did the door at the party for The Rapture!" The Rapture party! The nightmare of that evening comes flooding back to Thomas. . . . the pouring rain . . . the gunfight in the club . . . security trying to get Debbie Harry in past the unruly, drenched mob.

"Oh god, that bad?!" Thomas asks.

"They threatened to shoot us . . . they threatened to kill us!" Autumn wails. "Security had to rush us out of the lobby and into the tent. They locked the doors behind us." Suddenly, Erin, an intern for MAO, comes through the backstage door. "You guys have to see this. There's a big *hole* between the two tents!" he announces. "People from the Phat Farm show actually cut a hole in the tent so they could sneak into the Baby Phat show!"

"Good grief!" Brian says. "I should have stayed in retail." Just then Mauricio comes racing through the door. "Okay guys, we have to leave. *Now.*" *Oh god,* Thomas is thinking, *what next?* Mauricio shuttles the whole group outside and into a waiting car which speeds back toward MAO PR's office. No one says anything about the hasty getaway during the ride, but the reason is clear: there were a lot of disgruntled people— from angry editors to armed thugs—who did not get into the show and who were still milling around the tent. "I just didn't think it was a good idea that we hung around there any longer" is all Mauricio says, beads of sweat dripping from his forehead. Thomas can't stop thinking about the thugs and their guns.

Back at the office everyone is nursing a beer and retelling their war stories. "Does anyone have Valium?" someone asks. "Uh-oh" Mauricio says, looking at the answering machine. "There's a message." The general silent consensus seems to be: It's a death threat. Mauricio hesitantly reaches for the machine and presses *play.* "Hey Mauricio, it's Heather and Maggie from *Vogue*. . . . We just want you to know that we did *not* get into the Baby Phat show and we'll be talking to you soon." Her voice sounds very testy. She then adds coldly: "Have a good night." Click. Everyone in the room is silent for a few seconds. Autumn is staring at the answering machine in disbelief. "Uhm, hello? Earth to *Vogue*. We almost *died*."

Everyone bursts out laughing.

3 .

t's a rainy April night in Manhattan and Thomas is holding a clipboard and a broken umbrella as he surveys the long line of drenched, mostly white kids in camouflage trucker hats, quilted hunting jackets, denim overalls, even a few T-shirts with gun silhouettes printed on them. One young man, who is wearing a "Don't Mess with Texas" T-shirt, is frowning intently. The gathering resembles a group of drowned hillbilly rats. "What is this, a party for the National Rifle Association?" Thomas quips sarcastically to one of the bouncers. "I'm shocked that Charlton Heston isn't on the list." The event is a private party for the skateboard brand, Etnies, at a newly-opened club in the West Village called Movida. Because the dual-level club is the size of two Manhattan studio apartments, guests who have arrived late are being made to wait. And they're not happy about it. "But my boyfriend is in there waiting for me," insists a platinum-haired Asian girl who is wearing a T-shirt with "Ghe Tto Lux Ury" printed in four stacked,

[47]

gold foil quasi-syllables down the front. "And he's the assistant hat designer for Etnies."

"Well, why don't you call him and ask him to come out here?" Thomas says judiciously. "So we can be sure he's really here?" The girl groans and moves against the building, in an attempt to escape further drenching, and pulls a pink cell phone out of her gold quilted handbag. A gust of wind blows Thomas's umbrella inside out. "Shit!" As he struggles to pull it back, right side in, a visibly soused woman bumps into him, almost knocking his clipboard out of his hand. "Excuuuse me!" she bellows at Thomas. "That guy over there said I can't come in because I don't have my ID with me and he said I should talk to you."

"Well, what do you want me to do about it?" Thomas asks her testily. "Call you a cab so you can go home and find your driver's license?"

"Hey, I have to get up at five A.M. and teach in the morning, okay? I'm a school teacher," the woman slurs. "Cut me some slack and let me come in." The man in the Texas tee shoots her a deadly glance and tries to inch his way past her toward Thomas. "I'm sorry, no, you need to have some form of valid ID," Thomas tells her as she opens her purse and begins rifling through it. A prescription bottle falls out and pops open as it hits the sidewalk in front of Thomas's feet. "Goddamn it!" the woman howls as dozens of tiny white pills roll out and begin melting rapidly in the rain. "Ma'am, I'm terribly sorry, but you need to move away from the ropes. You're in everyone's way,"

Thomas tells her. The woman scoops up the pill bottle and turns to Thomas, her wet hair now matted against her forehead and cheek. "You're a very bad person and I would never stoop to your level!" she shrieks.

"Is it time to go home yet?" Thomas says wearily, turning to one of the bouncers.

Why would anyone want to be a doorman? What sort of person would endure crowds of obnoxious drunks, unruly thugs, and self-entitled yuppies? Who wants to deal with inclement weather, being on your feet all night, and risking assault by disgruntled night crawlers? What kind of person wants to wake up at noon after a hard night of crowd control and bull-shit dodging? And once you've decided that you're steel-nerved enough to deal with all of these job hazards, how do you get into the field and become the man who everyone wants out-side at the front of their club? How does someone get to be New York's Number-One Door Bitch?

"I'm like Linda Evangelista—I'm always professional and I'm always on time," jokes Thomas. "Actually the reality is, one of the main reasons I got into this is because I needed a job, I needed the money. A big chunk of my income comes from my doorman jobs." But there are plenty of *sensible* jobs to be had in New York, right? Why choose a profession that involves the diplomatic and ruthless sorting out of members of the in-crowd, the has-beens, the never-weres? "I guess it's something I've always had a passion for, from the time I was fifteen and living in New Jersey," says Thomas, who was an archetypal geek while in high school. Raised in the upper-middle-class suburb of Verona, Thomas read about the New York nightlife scene in magazines such as *Details* and *Interview*. He was especially a fan of Michael Alig's fanzine *Project X*, which featured outrageous and uncensored articles and photos from the decadent world of the club kids, from such venues as Tunnel, Area, Palladium, Limelight, and MK. Like many teens all over America, Thomas saw the club kids—equipped with outlandish outfits and shockingly amoral pronouncements—make regular appearances on talk shows like *Geraldo*. "I thought they were the most genius thing I ever saw in my life." He also saw cult films shown at midnight screenings, like the 1982 classic *Liquid Sky*, which portrayed a group of new wave night owls in New York who are preyed upon by heroin and orgasm-addicted aliens. "New York City seemed like the coolest place on the planet to me," says Thomas, echoing the sentiment of thousands of kids who gravitated to the city and its subcultures since the days when Jim Morrison and Jimi Hendrix were puking in Greenwich Village bathrooms.

In 1992, when he was fifteen years old, he snuck into Michael Alig's Disco 2000 at Limelight with a fake ID and from that moment on "everything changed." "I'll never forget that first night in the New York club scene," Thomas recalls excitedly. "I met all the subcultural celebrities I had read about in magazines—Amanda Lapore, Richie Rich, Sophia Lamar, James St. James—and I knew I was finally with my people." Thomas was especially fascinated by one character in particular—the door person at Disco 2000, Kenny Kenny. "I loved watching Kenny work the doors at clubs. I was fascinated by the way he controlled crowds and the things he said. He was always working the most amazing looks—over-the-top drag queen tranny ensembles with teetering heels, outrageous wigs, hairnets, exaggerated makeup, the works," Thomas reminisces. "He also had the most amazing attitude." Now, when Thomas says "attitude" he doesn't mean Kenny always gave it his best, good old college try, or he was upbeat and sunny with a Mother Teresa-like mission to save starving club kids and third world ravers. He means Catherine Deneuve and David Bowie in *The Hunger* vampire attitude. A razor-sharp stiletto heel digging into your flesh attitude. Kenny threw withering glances and caustic barbs that would strike his victims like a blast of Agent Orange, leaving them burned and disfigured for life—or until they bought a new outfit and made it past the ropes on their next try. "He was very loud, very aggressive, very mean," says Thomas. "He would say things like, 'What are you doing with that skirt on, darling, you look like a tourist. Step out of line!' He was ruthless. One night at Disco 2000, the mob at the door had really gotten out of hand and Kenny started screaming at everyone, 'If you all don't back up RIGHT NOW I'm eighty-sixing you all RIGHT OUT OF THIS LINE!' and a few people cried out 'But we're on the guest list!' and Kenny shouted back 'The guest list is CLOSED. I AM the guest list!' And I just loved that! He had

**THE TOP FIVE EXCUSES PEOPLE GIVE
FOR WHY IT SHOULD BE**

**1. "BUT MY FRIEND TOLD ME I
WAS ON THE GUEST LIST."** Many
would-be VIPs offer vague stories that run along the lines of
"My friend is friends with this
guy, the one who works at that
other club, and he said my
name would on the list tonight." A word of advice: If you
are one of these people, try doing a little research on the
names involved with the party
so you can at least produce a
semibelievable lie.

2. "I WORK HERE." This will usually prompt the door bitch to reply: "Great! Go strap on an
apron and help the bartender
wash out some glasses."

**3. "MAYBE IT'S UNDER MY CLUB
NAME."** Examples: Miranda
Moondust, the Duchess of

Continued

to act that way in order to control all the chaos
at those doors."

Slowly, Thomas became intrigued by the persona of the New York club doorman and began
standing outside of clubs all over the city, watching these imperious gatekeepers, these chic Cer-
beruses, lord over the seething, hedonistic masses.
There was the demented James St. James, who
later went on to pen *Disco Bloodbath,* the fashionable Kitty Boots, who famously gave Madonna a
five-dollar discount instead of VIP star treatment
at Jackie 60, and Darrell Elmore who worked the
ropes at Tunnel on West Twenty-seventh Street.
"Darrell was different, he was like the *austere*
doorman. He was always in a beautiful, well-
tailored dark suit, and then he'd have a full face of
foundation, with lip gloss, eyeliner . . . always a
very 'pressed' face. He was very standoffish and
would just stand there solemnly with his hands
folded, staring at you," Thomas recalls. "He was
very tough with people, even people who were
regulars at Tunnel. He would make them wait
forever and a day to get in . . . I didn't always
completely understand his logic. He also had
some great one-liners—like, if someone tried to
sneak across the ropes he'd say 'This is my land,
and that is yours.' I loved every second of it."

Thomas spent about three years watching these club land conductors—until he was eighteen—and it was then that he began considering the doorman profession for himself. "I started thinking this could be one of those 'cool jobs' that people had, sort of like being an agent for the FBI or working as a fashion editor, deciding who and what appears on magazine covers," says Thomas. "A doorperson gets to decide who gets in and who doesn't—what could be cooler than that?"

It was a typically sweaty night in the summer of 1997 at Don Hill's, the Soho club that hosted a night called Squeezebox—which had a vibe that combined the raw punk energy of early CBGB's and the 'eighties drag queen iconoclasm of the Pyramid Club—during most of the 'nineties. The club's MC, an acid-tongued drag queen with a dominatrixlike demeanor named Misstress Formika, was singing her rendition of Hole's "Violet" with the Squeezebox band as a crowd of tattooed rocker boys and girls of all sexual stripes threw themselves around the dance floor. It was this night that Thomas met Martin Belk, the producer and technology direc-

Razzle Dazzle, Tommy Hott Pants, Hedda Lettuce, Butros Butros-Ghali, etc. The more outrageous and ridiculous your club name is—whether you're telling the truth or not—the greater your chances are of getting into the club. Additional tip: If you're fabricating a club name, a minor adjustment to your physical appearance—such as shaving off your eyebrows, tattooing "Human Ashtray" on your upper lip or wearing nothing but a red satin jockstrap and devil horns—will increase your credibility.

4. "I DON'T NEED TO BE ON THE LIST, THIS IS MY FRIEND'S PARTY." Instead of insisting they're on the list, some people will use this excuse as a form of reverse psychology. Tip: Sometimes it's better to just cough up the five- or ten-dollar entrance fee and spare yourself humiliation at the hands of the door bitch.

5. "MY PUBLICIST/AGENT/ASSISTANT/PERSONAL SHOPPER FAXED IN A REQUEST—DIDN'T YOU

Continued

RECEIVE IT?" "No, but if you have a note from your mommy, I might let you in," is a common door bitch retort.

tor of the club, and was plucked out of the crowd and recruited to do promotion for the polysexual rock 'n' roll party.

Belk recalls: "I was hanging out by the back bar with Michael Schmidt, the creator of Squeezebox, and he pointed Thomas out to me, saying he had heard he was studying public relations at NYU and he might be a good person to help us promote the club. This was at a point where things were really taking off. There was a lot of stuff going on: I was working with Joey Ramone trying to help organize his birthday gig, Debbie Harry—who often performed at the club—was putting Blondie back together, legendary performers like Nina Hagen, Lena Lovich, Marc Almond, and Courtney Love were doing shows on our stage, we were doing live Internet broadcasts and getting lots of press. It was a very busy time and we needed someone's help, and we decided to give Thomas a try.

"At the beginning, I couldn't tell if he was truly a *keeper*, in the sense of a fellow rock and roll hag, or not. Like the rest of us in the 'outcast' scene—rocker fags and freaks who didn't care for the vapid, mainstream gay party circuit—he was yet another lost puppy looking for his spot on the carpet. I think Thomas was understandably cautious before diving in head first with an eccentric, unpredictable, and sometimes volatile group of people. Problem was, it was incredibly difficult finding people worth a crap. Most of them were hangers-on who didn't really want to work. The rest of them just wanted to hang around us and the rock stars, or would use a promotional gig—handing out flyers for Squeezebox at other venues—just as a way to convince us to let them get up on stage and perform. So, by sheer luck of him being in the right place at the right time, I started hiring Thomas for small jobs—flyering, faxing, press releases, and store promotions."

People who run night clubs tend to be a vain, distrustful, and internecine lot, and there was at least one Squeezebox kingpin who wasn't entirely convinced of Thomas's worthiness—Patrick Briggs. An Iggy Pop–like performer who fronted a short-lived glam rock band called Psychotica and an organizer for Lollapalooza, Patrick projected the kind of rock star attitude and aloofness that was generally reserved for more bonafide celebrities. This sort of self-aggrandizing stance has always been a common syndrome in New York nightlife and, to the schadenfreude delight of many, often leads to the demise of said stars—in this case, a rapid fall accelerated by drug abuse and exile from the club scenes in both New York and L.A. But that's, as they say, life in the Big City. At the time Patrick met Thomas, Patrick was precipitously elevated on his rock and roll high horse. "Briggs was completely ambivalent about Thomas," remembers Belk. "It was very 'Hi, Bye' with Patrick. He was always reserved with new people in the inner circle. We'd already gotten burned a couple of times by people making big promises and not keeping them—all the while using our hard-earned cache to further their own agenda. But Thomas was able to win even Patrick over."

After a few months of doing promotions for Squeezebox, Thomas started setting his sights higher. "We had meetings where Michael Schmidt would talk about things that he thought would enliven the party and bring it back—because it was losing its luster—and make it a little stronger," Thomas remembers. When Squeezebox first started, the club employed a door girl named Lauren Pine, famous for her extremely corseted waist and bubbly demeanor, who drew the right crowd as a result of word-of-mouth in the chic rocker community. But when she left to pursue a career in the medical field, the crowd slowly began to change.

"For a time we didn't have a real doorman. Don Hill would sit out there and take people's money and check people off the guest list and it was okay because he knows everybody. But then he stopped doing the door and we didn't have a real doorman, there were just bouncers taking people's money," explains Belk. "Then one night Michael Schmidt was home sick and I didn't manage to get the guest list from him and people made asses of themselves at the door over ten bucks. That's when I realized we needed a real presence."

Soon there were people showing up at the club who appeared to be bland, middle-class matrons and slumming stockbrokers, and the club's cool cachet started to dwindle. Despite the fact that bourgeois fashion designer Isaac Mizrahi made an appearance at the club and clumsily pronounced it "the sort of place that someone might get shot at" in the press, Squeezebox was starting to lack a bit of the razor-sharp edge that made it immensely popular in the beginning. Thomas was determined to bring that back by returning some rock 'n' roll attitude to the door.

"I wanted to do that job so badly, so I basically campaigned for myself," says Thomas. "I went up to everyone separately—Michael, Patrick, this guy Ronnie who was involved with booking the bands—and made a pitch that the club should give me a try as the new doorman. I was studying public relations at NYU at the time, so I was thinking in that frame of mind—pitching myself like I was a proposal or a project. But they were really unsure about me. They said 'it's a really crappy job and a lot of people will end up not liking you because you couldn't let them in for free,' and they were considering other people for the job. But eventually they caved in and let me try out the job for one night."

"When I first met Thomas, he was a young kid—bright, eager, and perhaps a bit aloof," says Michael Schmidt, the fashion and accessories designer who conceived and founded Squeezebox in 1994. "All of these qualities together help make for an ideal doorperson, as you want an energetic person who can manage an unruly crowd, a rambling guest list, and a tightly wound security detail all at once, all night long. But they must also be able to remain detached from the people who would try to schmooze them for complimentary admission. It's crucial to the success of a club that your doorperson makes people pay to get in, otherwise you can't pay your people at the end of the night—including your doorperson!"

A veteran of the New York nightclub scene, Schmidt knows of what he speaks. His resume includes having designed for Cher, Tina Turner, Iggy Pop, Ozzy Osbourne, Madonna, Jenna Jameson, and a slew of metal bands. His razor blade dress for Debbie Harry is a punk couture classic, and he was roommates with both Cher and Harry in L.A. and New York, respectively. In the early 'nineties he designed the VIP room of the cavernous club, Palladium, which included walls that changed color when they sensed heat, and the lyrics to Iggy Pop's "Nightclubbing" spelled out in Braille with metal studs that he nailed into the floor.

At Squeezebox he was always the belle of the ball, treating everyone like a VIP, proffering complimentary cocktails and graciously introducing celebrities to everyone who wanted to meet them. He was never without his Chanel compact, a nude-lipsticked smile, and a hilarious story from the world of rock style. "A person's nightlife is important to them simply because it's the antithesis of their day life," says Schmidt. "We all need to find a balance in our lives between the drudgery of jobs and school, and the time we spend with friends. Nightclubs facilitate this. You go out to clubs to see fun people and dance and blow off a little steam. . . . and this place becomes important to you, and you want to protect it from interlopers. This is the job of a doorperson. They are the filter through which you must pass into another, perhaps more exotic and entertaining world. A really good doorperson will keep the quality level high by allowing delicious and interesting people inside and sending gawkers on their way."

Schmidt remembers well Thomas's first night at the door. "He really kept his cool and the club did well, Thomas really contributed to the growth of the club. I had the impression that it was more than just a job for him—he really believed in what we were trying to accomplish at Squeezebox, and he quickly became a crucial member of the family. His taste level is quite high. Thomas can quickly discern between those who really contribute to a scene and those who just feed off it. But he's not just a monolith placed at the gates to the kingdom to intimidate trespassers; he's elegant, very welcoming, and smooth. After all, you don't want too many people running screaming into the night after being humiliated by a doorperson—they might get hit by a cab."

Thomas has proud memories of his first night at the door. "I was definitely thinning the crowd out a bit, and the club had more of the energy and the mix that it had in the beginning. I decided who got in for free and who had to pay five dollars or ten dollars. Being that it was my first doorman job and I was still a bit green, there were nights when I didn't recognize a certain magazine editor or friend of a performer, etcetera, and there were times when I wasn't sure if I had done the right thing." One particularly crowded night, in the spring of 1998, Thomas was in the midst of checking in a group of five people who were on the guest list when actress and fashion muse Chloe Sevigny showed up at the door. "This was before the film *Boys Don't Cry* came out, but I definitely knew who she was, I had been seeing her out at clubs since I was fifteen, but I didn't really know her personally—we weren't B. F. F. and we weren't having brunch, but we had chatted briefly a couple of times at parties.

So I turned to her and said 'Hey, how are you? I'm just checking in this group before you, hold on a sec,' and she sort of muscled her way in front of the group and said to me 'But I'm with Alexander McQueen.' Well, I didn't notice McQueen because he's kind of short, so I looked behind her and the group of five and I saw him standing there and I was so aggravated by Chloe's behavior that I said 'Thanks, I'm aware of that.' Yes, it was a bit curt, but it was a very busy night and she caught me at the wrong moment. And I thought it was so uncool that she had to drop someone else's name, the name of the famous person she was with, especially since it was so obvious that I knew who she was. Now mind you, at this point in my life, I *worshipped* Alexander McQueen. I thought he was a fashion genius. I had all the clippings, and I even had the cover of *The Face,* featuring him, taped to my wall at home. But I remained aloof and professional, and when I was done with the group of five, I turned to Chloe and Alexander, who had about three friends with them. 'Okay Chloe, I can comp you and Alexander but your friends each have to pay ten dollars.'

"Well, Chloe was furious and her friends got very huffy. When Chloe got inside the club she found Michael Schmidt and immediately began complaining about me, I think she even wanted to have me fired. A few minutes later, Schmidt popped his head out and I was like 'Oh boy, here goes, I'm in trouble now,' and before he said anything I said, a bit defensively, 'For what it's worth, I comped them but charged their friends. I know Chloe and she was so rude to me,' and Michael said 'Good! I'm glad you charged them!' I mean, at the end of the day, we're in a money-making venture here and you can't let everyone in for free.

"A few years later I got to know Chloe and I think she's amazing," Thomas continues. "She's very smart and she's a terrific actress. I loved her performance in *Melinda and Melinda*. She has a very natural ability."

During his tenor at Squeezebox, Thomas started getting in touch with his glam rock 'n' roll side: he began sporting severe makeup and hairstyles, fashionable rocker ensembles, and glitter, lots of glitter. "Thomas came to the scene with a sense of glamour and absorbed the rest from the extended crowd of glam people," says Belk. "He is one of the few who understands that the entrance to a good club is the apex of the glam, the liminal act of taking something challenging, ugly, or limiting—your looks, your job, your life—and making it beautiful, sexy, and new. I think I could take an ounce of credit for being the one who helped Thomas get in touch with his sparkly side. Thomas recognizes and acknowledges the glam efforts people make, and that's why he's remembered and sought after as a doorman."

As Squeezebox wound to a close other doorman opportunities started popping up for Thomas. Misstress Formika started hosting a rock 'n' roll party at a dark, mazelike fire trap called Kitsch Inn on Twenty-third Street. Kitsch Inn was a boozy, loud den where lean, scruffy boys in makeup and the girls (and other boys) who love them fraternized on moldy sofas while listening to live performers and what was categorized as "kitschy" rock music: Twisted Sister, Def Leppard, Dolly Parton, and the Monkees rounded out the DJ sets. Thomas was hired to man their ropes by Formika and Abby Ehmann, a rock promoter and member of the group Feminists for Free Expression, who published a 'zine called *Porn Free*. Ehmann, who is known in downtown New York circles for her sex and fetish parties, began throwing the Kitsch Inn party because of her soft spot for heavy metal hair bands, and she thought Thomas would be the right person to have at their door. "We liked him because he can be tough without being a dick," says Ehmann, who is credited with giving Thomas the nickname "Door Bitch." "Thomas was so visible at all the fun, downtown parties that he became the first person people think of when they think 'doorperson,' much as Kenny Kenny used to be."

"The nickname 'Door Bitch' and the reputation that came with it became a myth that sort of perpetuated itself," explains Thomas. "I never set out to be a bitch. As long as people are polite, I'll be polite right back to them. Unfortunately, in the world of nightlife—where people are drunk, stoned, self-entitled, ego-bloated, or just plain angry—there isn't always a Miss Manners code of conduct happening. I have to be a bitch sometimes to keep things in line. But you won't see me sending out press releases stating I'm a self-proclaimed door bitch." Once the word got out that Thomas was New York's newest and most visible door bitch, the nickname caught on, and the media—*The Village Voice, Spin,* and various New York party magazines—seized upon it, built it up, and exaggerated his reputation as a door tyrant. As Sylvia Plath once wrote "every woman adores a fascist," so every sensationalistic journalist and catty club-hopper adores a bitch. "It's just the way my personality is, especially when I'm at work and I have to turn on the doorman persona. I have to be on and paying attention and telling people what to do and 'are you on the guest list—how many are you?' I have to be on the ball," says Thomas. "I may be a Pisces but I have a Virgo rising and a Virgo moon. My yin and yang are Virgo, okay? So that accounts for my overwhelming need to do a great job, to be in control . . . to be the dictator."

Michael T., founder of the roving rock party Motherfucker and self-styled tastemaker, sometimes loses track of the conversation. "This white suit I'm wearing was based on a Bowie getup from 1973. It's the outfit he wears while singing "Sorrow" to

Amanda Lear on the 1980 TV special *Floor Show.* Real sick, gorgeous stuff . . . you'll *never* see that on television today!" he enthuses, as he slides the original vinyl pressing of *Diamond Dogs* out of its plastic protective sleeve and places it gingerly on the turntable in the Mofo DJ booth. He then remembers that he had been speaking about Thomas. "Do you want to know how Thomas became such an in-demand doorman? This party, Motherfucker, that's how! Huge lines to get in, with him picking people out of the crowd or throwing people off the line—that was unheard of at a rock 'n' roll party. Who in their right mind wouldn't notice that? Thomas is our head doorman and people paid attention to him immediately. We put the Door Bitch on the map!" Michael and his partners, George Seville, Johnny T., and Justine D., first hired Thomas to do the door to their party on New Year's Eve 2000–2001. "I had known Thomas from Squeezebox and noticed that he had started to cultivate this door persona and I thought it might work for what we were trying to do, although I did have some reservations," Michael continues. "I thought that Thomas the 'door bitch' might be *too* bitchy, which could be a bit of a turn-off to the young faces of the time who might not have been aware of Squeezebox or just that type of personality at the door. My partners and I discussed it and we decided that Thomas's knowledge of our scene, the music, and the fashion, plus his general enthusiasm, was worth taking the risk." And as it turned out, the Door Bitch was worth the risk and Mother-fucker has become the biggest rock 'n' roll party in America.

"Thomas is quite sociable and savvy—those are the two ingredients for a *good* doorperson. Thomas is also quick and can be quite pleasant, but also quite sharp with his tongue when necessary—to say the least."

"Remember when glitter made everything better?" Thomas asks rhetorically, between spoonfuls of the Peanut Butter Bomb cake he is shoveling into his mouth. He is lunching with a friend on a late Saturday afternoon at Teany—an inconspicuously hip café on the Lower East Side, which is owned by musician and social walker Moby. "Do you ever wonder if you've gravitated toward the doorman profession because the door is the only place in your life where you have control?" his friend asks. Thomas finishes chewing the last gooey chunk of cake before he answers. "I've never really thought about it," he says, seeming a bit flustered. Just then Moby walks in, spots Thomas, and walks over to say hi.

"Hey Mo, how's it going," Thomas says after wiping the circle of crumbs and peanut butter from his mouth.

"I'm good, how are the velvet ropes treating you? Sorry I missed the last Motherfucker party—how was it?" he asks as he makes his way toward the kitchen.

"It was amazing, you missed the party of the year. You should definitely try to make it to the next one." Moby disappears into the kitchen and Thomas turns back to his friend who is still waiting for an answer. "Well, obviously in certain aspects of my life I don't have as much control as I do when I'm working the door," Thomas says slowly. "There are other aspects of my professional life where I'm becoming successful, like my other gig working as a freelance fashion show producer, and I also have really great friends . . . but then there are areas of my life where, yes, maybe I don't have control, like I have a really crappy love life or I'm fat or I have body dysmorphic issues."

"Your addiction to porn," his friend adds helpfully.

"Thanks for that, doll. But give me a break—who has perfect control in every aspect of their life? Almost nobody—not even Oprah or Tony Robbins! But then again, my choice to be a doorman was proactive. I saw an arena where I had control."

"Don't you think that sometimes people see your tyrannical attitude at the door as a revenge scenario? Maybe the people you turn away at the door remind you of the kids who picked on you in school?"

"Well, a lot of people I turn away at the door, let's be totally honest—I'm not friends with a lot of people like them—it's not my crowd, it's not my scene. I don't really know who they are, they just look really mainstream."

"Maybe they're just slightly older versions of your 'hipster' friends who have turned in their checkered Van sneakers and skinny jeans for Brooks Brothers shirts, and have trimmed their bangs to a respectable length?"

"No, they're more the sort of people who I grew up with in the suburbs. I like to call them 'young, self-entitled white people," Thomas says, starting to sound a little angry. "They have decent corporate jobs and huge egos, and can't understand why their money can't buy them anything they want, and they can't understand why their status can't get them into the clubs where I work. They're young, egocentric, self-entitled white kids and they think New York is one big episode of *Sex and the City* . . . they're all fucking ridiculous!"

"Calm down, door terminator, I'm sure they'll get their just desserts—and it won't be a Peanut Butter Bomb."

"And as Penny Arcade says in her monologues: 'The kids who are popular in high school are never popular in adulthood.' Now, I have to go home and start getting ready for MisShapes."

"Okay. Do you need any help carrying your weapons of mainstream destruction to the club?"

"Very funny—you're a regular Carrot Top. Just come by around four A.M. and bring me a Peanut Butter Bomb."

"You got it, Mein Herr door bitch."

4 .

A seven-foot-tall drag queen is standing on the perimeter of the dance floor in a small bi-level club in the West Village, towering over a sweaty gathering of twenty-somethings. With her blonde bubble-do wig, red miniskirt, gaudy costume jewelry, elbow gloves, and stiletto sandals, the queen looks like she's just stepped out of the chorus line of a rendition of "Big Spender" from the moldy musical *Sweet Charity*. But instead of the brassy, bombastic strains of a Cy Coleman chestnut, the kids in checkered Vans sneakers, stovepipe trousers, striped, asymmetrical skirts, and sheer and shredded mesh tees, are hopping around to a doom-laden dance track. Almost as moldy as Bob Fosse fodder, the song—"Love Will Tear Us Apart," from gloomy British band Joy Division—was released in 1980, a few years before most of the people in this crowd were even born. The drag queen remains frozen—not even attempting a wooden swivel of her miniskirted hips—and the cocktail she is clutching looks naked without a colored paper umbrella.

WHAT COSTUMES WILL THE COOL KIDS WEAR?
A STYLE GUIDE TO ALL TOMORROW'S PARTIES

INDIE ROCKERS
Who Are They? The Indie Rockers are kids in their early-to-midtwenties who listened to "indie" rock during their formative years in the mid-to-late 'nineties—Nirvana, Hole, Smashing Pumpkins, Sonic Youth, Pulp, Blur, Oasis, Suede—and have basically never stopped listening to it.

The Look. A bit casual—blazers over T-shirts, low-rider jeans, vintage jeans, old-school sneakers such as Converse, Adidas, Vans (see also "'80s New Wavers") and maybe a bit of a British lad influence, minus the excess testosterone (athletic clothing, Fred Perry polos, mesh soccer tops). Indie rock hair styles include shaved heads, hair gelled into dorsal fins, long bangs, mop tops, and mullets. Many have copped their style from The Strokes— skinny jeans, Converse sneakers, shaggy hair—who in turn copped their look from The

Continued

GLENN BELVERIO

The scene is a weekly dance party called Mis-Shapes, and it's named after a song by late-'nineties Britpop band Pulp. "Mis-shapes, mistakes, misfits/Raised on a diet of broken biscuits, oh, we don't look the same as you." Outside, Thomas guards the ropes to this small, exclusive club, with his style radar turned up to its highest surveillance setting. It's doubtful that the young crowd of hipsters waiting to get in was raised on "broken biscuits," but a good portion of the boys and girls are so thin that one can't help wondering if youthful metabolism or the legacy of Kate Moss is responsible. Lacking the graceful carriage or seasoned demeanor of a typical New York society dweller, the white, middle-class youths are slightly awkward in their slender bodies, like a contingent of teenaged Protestant choir members after a few forbidden cocktails. "Do *both* of you have backstage passes?" Thomas asks, sounding like an impatient school marm grilling her students about permission notes from their parents. He is referring to a rock concert that took place earlier this evening in Central Park, and only people with passes are being admitted into the packed club at the moment. A gangly boy in a Sex Pistols T-shirt explains how they were issued only one pass for both him and his girlfriend. The girlfriend—who sports a tall, heavily-gelled faux hawk, dangling green plastic heart-shaped earrings and a 'fifties-style cocktail dress with a Twister Board–like print—wears a worried expression. "Well, we are full to capacity now and one pass won't get you both in," Thomas tells them sternly. They move over to the curb and the boy looks like he's going to burst into tears. The girl pulls at the front of her slick hairdo, seeming equally concerned about gravity ruining her look as she is about not getting into the club.

Each week the MisShapes party features guest DJs, many of them famous or semi-famous—Kelly Osbourne, Carlos D. of Interpol, Dior Homme designer Hedi Slimane—and unknown kids who meet the MisShapes criteria for "good taste in music." This week the club is hosting an after party for a concert by The Killers, a neo-new-wave band that is part of a movement of "new rock" acts. Like many of the acts, The Killers bear an uncanny resemblance to the glut of flash-in-the-pan, prefabricated bands—Duran Duran imitators mostly—that cropped up throughout the 'eighties. The lead singer of The Killers, Brandon Flowers, is spin-

Ramones. The Indie Rocker look is mainly the province of the male of the hipster species; unfortunately, the girls aren't brave enough to bring back baby doll lingerie, tiaras, smeared lipstick, and barbiturates abuse.

Pavlovian Response: "Celebrity Skin" by Hole, or "Girls and Boys" by Blur comes on and the Indie Rockers start partying like it's 1999.

Diagnosis: Like hippies who lingered well into the 'seventies with their long hair and peace sign amulets, the Indie Rockers have the feel of college graduates who still haven't outgrown their teen or preteen years. They may think they still smell like teen spirit, but they are now old enough to drink legally, hold down jobs as graphic designers, and recommend the correct organic, low-fat diet and Pilates regiment for Courtney Love.

Advertising/Marketing Potential: A lot. Old-school sneakers are all the rage.

Continued

The Door Bitch's Decree: "I want to be the guy with the most cake . . . someday they will ache like I ache."

PUNKS
Who Are They?
Kids who look like they were abducted from King's Road in London or St. Mark's Place in New York City in 1979 and cryogenically frozen. For whatever reason, punk is one of those resilient youth styles that refuses to roll over and die. It's a look that's as classic as a Chanel suit or a little black dress. The new punk kids are a lot more open-minded about music than their predecessors—mainly because it's difficult to dance to "Louie Louie" by Black Flag without seriously injuring someone—and worship at the altar of vintage Vivienne Westwood . . . even though the jaded designer would probably cross the street to avoid them.

The Look: Skinny, plaid bondage pants, sleeveless T-shirts—The Exploited, Dead Kennedys, the Misfits (the one with the gi-

Continued

ning music from the tiny DJ booth that overlooks the jam-packed second-story dance floor. Dressed in a white peak lapel blazer over a black polo top, Flowers is known for courting controversy by pairing makeup—tonight he's wearing eye shadow, mascara, and pink lipstick—with his outspoken identity as a Mormon. While his religious background prohibits him from being at a club where alcohol, premarital sex—surreptitious copulation behind the ice machine has become a MisShapes rite of passage—and homosexuals are in evidence, Flower's presence fails to draw hurled lightning bolts upon the venue. Even if that were to happen, the kids—inured to both calculated controversy and divine retribution—are way too busy dancing. It's safe to assume they have stronger opinions regarding music than organized religion.

"A lot of kids don't feel that the music that is being made now is to going to stand up like 'eighties music does," says Thomas, who, as doorman of MisShapes since its inception in February 2004, is both an expert on the kids who come to the party and the contemporary music scene in general. "There are bands from the 'eighties that were one-hit wonders, but I think there are even more bands now that will

[72]

not last." While the DJs at MisShapes play a fairly wide array of music—indie rock like Hole and Oasis, newer bands like the Yeah Yeah Yeahs and Franz Ferdinand, and even some pop dance music—a lot of the kids who come to Mis-Shapes, who are in the twenty-one-to-twenty-six age range, have a fanatical devotion to late-'seventies and 'eighties music and style. Thomas, having been that type of retro fan when he was a teenager and older, knows this phenomenon well.

"There is a small, yet loyal group of kids who come to this party who are music *freaks.* They're total music nerds and they're kind of snobby. They've done exhaustive research into music from that era by reading tons of books, like *Please Kill Me* and *Post Punk Diary,* they've looked up stuff on the Internet about the Mudd Club and CBGB's and they know all the bands and every song, from the hits to obscure B-sides. And with that they've studied the clothing—looking at thousands of photos of punks and new wavers, and they've come to romanticize this whole period that they were too young to be a part of. As a result, MisShapes has a certain air of elitism about it, these kids are a bit stuck-up about the fact that they consider themselves

ant skull motif)—"brothel creeper" shoes, spiked leather collars, belts, and wristbands. Hairdos—mohawks, big spikes, dyed colors. Their girlfriends and/or fag hags are more in the Siouxsie Sioux vein (see "goths").

Pavlovian Response: They want to dance to The Clash but they'll settle for Bloc Party.

Diagnosis: Even though it was more effective in 1977, when newspapers screamed head-lines like "Punk Rock Men-ace!", these kids are pleased to have a "rebellious" lifestyle to plunder that sufficiently an-noys their parents . . . except this time the parents are irri-tated by their offsprings' lack of originality.

Advertising/Marketing Potential: Some. There's nothing like the visual one-liner of a punk in-serted in the background of a beer commercial.

The Door Bitch's Decree: "I would love to invite Vivienne West-wood to the club and have her

Continued

[73]

meet these kids . . . if she would only return our calls."

meet these kids . . . if she
would only return our calls."

meet these kids . . . if she would only return our calls."

FASHIONISTAS

Who Are They? Girls and boys who are into high fashion and glamour or just the latest trends. This crew devours magazines like *i-D, V, Nylon, Vogue, Harper's Bazaar, Lucky,* and *Cargo,* and pay close attention to the latest fashions. They either duplicate or reinterpret the looks they see in the magazines—whether they can afford to buy the real stuff, do it on the cheap, or compose a combination of both. The more advanced of this species, referred to as "ironauts", or early adapters, are ostensibly ahead of the trends, sporting clothes and accessories that haven't hit the mass market yet.

The Look: The latest fashions bought and/or charged at Barney's, Barney's Co-Op, Seven, Atelier, Opening Ceremony, Kirna Zabete, Madison Avenue boutiques. Similar styles might be found at H & M for a

Continued

experts on this era of music and style. Then there are the kids who come to the club who copy the ones who have really done their homework—one of the less well-read ones might be wearing a ripped T-shirt held together with a couple of safety pins because he saw someone else wearing one, not knowing that Richard Hell is the one credited with spearheading this look back in 1975. And then there is the more obvious snobbery that is a part of MisShapes, the other kids who are merely elitist about being young, skinny, and tattooed, and about the fact that they can get into MisShapes every week."

"MisShapes is like a utopian high school cafeteria," declares Leigh Lezark, one of the three founders of the party. "It's for everybody; people from all these scenes congregate and they all get along." Leigh is the twenty-one-year-old girl member of the trio who, after their party, call themselves the MisShapes. She moved to New York from New Jersey when she was seventeen and now works as a model while dabbling in photography. She is flitting around the apartment of Greg.K, twenty-five, another member of the party-promoting collective.

The third member, Geo, is twenty-one and hails from Mississauga, Canada. He also moved to New York when he was seventeen, and, while he possesses a sort of Canadian aloofness, he is the most outspoken of the three. With his exaggerated, black mop top hairdo, he resembles one of the cartoon caricatures of Paul McCartney that appeared during the early years of The Beatles. "I don't think there are scenes anymore," he admonishes Leigh. "There's nothing that's an established party left in New York anymore, just mega-clubs for out-of-town people. Our club is packed every week, we've never lost our crowd . . . and we've been going for almost two years now." In the tradition of P. T. Barnum and just about every club promoter who has been around since the invention of the cocktail stirrer, Geo knows how to weave a mythology and a history before the narrative has even reached the midpoint of the story. Like any young creative person who comes to the big city and starts getting attention from the press for his efforts, Geo is imbued with a potent sensation of cultural significance and long-term invincibility.

But, as the MisShapes's predecessors know, newspaper articles become yellow with time, and there's always someone younger and hungrier right behind you. "We were influenced by the DJs who played at parties that we went to

fraction of the price and won't necessarily disqualify the wearer from the Fashionista species. Ironauts with showroom connections might be seen wearing items one season before they're available in stores. They also raid places like Patricia Field, or thrift stores, for trendsetting looks.

Pavlovian Response: Is that Chloe Sevigny and Carine Roitfeld who just walked in?

Diagnosis: While they sometimes come off as victims, this fashion-forward group is determined not to become mired in the past . . . unless Anna Wintour declares "being mired in the past" the next big thing, and then they're all over it before you can say "maxed-out Platinum card." They might scoff at a passé punk tartan kilt or a goth spider web shawl . . . until these items are seen on a model marching down a John Galliano runway on Style.com, and they've then preordered them from their inside connections.

Continued

Advertising/Marketing Potential: Incalculable. The Fashionistas are walking ads for the entire fashion industry, which is why the more prominent of the clan receive truckloads of swag from designers on a regular basis.

The Door Bitch's Decree: "I'm secretly a fashion addict, and I can tell the difference between Nicolas Ghesquiere for Balenciaga leather fringe, and thrift store fringe, on someone before they even get out of the cab. Fashionistas usually get in right away, unless they look like they've just rolled into Manhattan on the Hamptons Jitney. I want *Eyes of Laura Mars* fashionistas, not contrived *Sex and the City* fashion victims."

'80S NEW WAVERS Who Are They? Students of nostalgia who have studied the history of 'eighties music and style. They've seen *Desperately Seeking Susan*, *The Hunger*, *Liquid Sky*, *Ladies and Gentlemen, the Fabulous Stains*, and *24 Hour Party Peo-*

Continued

when we first came to New York," Geo says, referring to old-school club people such as Larry Tee and Michael T. "These DJs have faded into the background . . . those older nightlife figures are not as prominent in the New York club scene anymore. There are a couple left, but as far as DJs go, it's all new people, new parties . . . everything's new."

Or rather, everything that's old is new yet again. Tossed about on the postmodern sea, where waves of reference constantly crash against each other, today's kids are a mélange of styles that blend distant nostalgia, dated teenage sentimentality, and media savvy—and the Mis-Shapes are archetypal examples. "They're a combination of fashionista mixed with goth post punk, topped with a twist of early synth pop," Thomas says archly. "When they first contacted me to do the door to their party, I was interested because I really liked them, I thought they were cute—but I was also a bit wary. They're young, it was their first party, and I wasn't sure how messy they were in regards to their partying habits." At the time, Thomas had a steady door gig at a club called Coral Room, which drew a crowd of wannabe hip-hop kids who booked tables and showed off by buying two-hundred-plus-dollar bottles of alcohol for their friends. "It was a steady gig, but it was lame and I really wasn't into it," Thomas recalls. "So I took the plunge and left Coral Room to become the Mis-Shapes doorman, even though I wasn't sure if the party would be a success or if it would last longer than a few weeks. But the party took off in a big way after a month or two, so it worked out . . . and of course I love seeing all these great kids getting dressed up every week, working their looks, and making the party a special place to be."

MisShapes is a microcosm of 'noughties youth culture style statements. As virtually impossible as it is for a bona fide subculture to exist in a world where corporations employ armies of trend spotters—global style pirates armed with digital cameras—today's kids are dressing up with the same determination as those of generations past.

Now, why do these kids go to all this trouble of painting their faces, chasing trends, dumpster-diving for old Sham 69 T-shirts, and letting their bangs grow into their eyes? To get their photos taken, of course! "People come to the club to get their picture taken, usually," says Geo, who employs two digital photographers

ple hundreds of times and they own every album and single put out by The Cure, Visage, Soft Cell, Adam and the Ants, Tones on Tail, X-ray Specs, Missing Persons, Haysi Fantayzee, Sigue Sigue Sputnik, Gary Numan, Scritti Politti, and Toyah.

The Look: Off-the-shoulder *Flashdance* tops, lots of eyeliner and asymmetrical bangs over one eye (boys and girls), miniskirts, florescent colors, superwide belts, long, gaudy earrings, stiletto heels or brightly-colored pumps, punk/new wave T-shirts and/or lots of buttons (Blondie, Talking Heads, Devo, PiL, The Cramps), vintage Stephen Sprouse, skinny jeans, skinny ties, tight striped T-shirts and sneakers (Converse, checkered Vans) for the boys.

Pavlovian Response: "Hear this song that's playing now? I have the original purple and white marbleized vinyl twelve-inch single that was sold in a limited edition of fifty in 1983."

Continued

who roam through the crowd every week. "We document every single week and every single 'look' . . . and we post the best photos on our Web site. After we update each party, people visit the site so they can look at photos of themselves and their friends." Anyone who lives in places like New York or L.A. knows that clinical narcissism is no longer the province of actors, musicians, and politicians, and if there's one thing the kids of today live for, it's having their photos taken. The MisShapes Web site and other sites, such as Lastnightsparty.com, cater to funloving vanity cases who go out to parties every night and log on to the Web every day to inspect their tattoos, outfits, and faces—which are either carefully posed or twisted with drunkenness.

Spoiled by the instant gratification of digital photography and the blog explosion, the kids of today have no idea how difficult it was to be a fulfilled, nonfamous media whore before the dawn of the computerized age. Fifteen or twenty years ago, when a photographer took your picture at a club, it really meant something. It was a mini-moment of glory that only a select number experienced. The subject then hoped they would be lucky enough to appear in *Women's Wear Daily* or *Details* or *Interview* . . . sometimes

Diagnosis: The '80s New Wavers get high marks for actually having spent the time to research the history of the music. More than just retro trendoids, these geeks have committed years of their lives to absorbing a period of time that they consider to be the zenith of civilization. Like Trekkies who won't talk to anyone who doesn't speak fluent Romulan, these kids will look down their nose at anyone who doesn't know the lyrics to every song on *Dirk Wears White Sox.*

Advertising/Marketing Potential: Tons. All those consumers in their late thirties love a little nostalgia mixed in with their sales pitches: "Honey, you have to see this! There are peanut butter cups pogoing to "I Want Candy" by Bow Wow Wow on TV!"

The Door Bitch's Decree: "These kids know deep in their hearts that no one will be listening to My Chemical Romance or The Killers in twenty years, but hundreds of thousands of eighteen-year-olds will be sit-

Continued

waiting months to see if they were cropped out of a photo where they once stood next to Madonna's brother or a drag queen with a four-foot beehive hairdo. With the thousands of nightlife photos that pop up on the Web on a daily basis, that kind of photographic ego anxiety is a thing of the past. And, whereas the idealistic rock stars and purist punks of yore made a lot of noise about being antiestablishment, today's kids welcome the establishment with open arms . . . and hold on tight.

"This whole generation is so into getting their pictures taken," says Thomas. "The entire culture of the United States, in the last few years, has existed almost solely for celebrities. They are in every aspect of the culture—they are the beauties, the icons, the endorsers of every product. You can be at the lamest party in the world, but if Jessica Simpson shows up, it suddenly become the coolest thing ever. Today's kids, including the kids who come to MisShapes week after week, recognize that people with no talent can become extremely, globally famous, and they see the photos of these people everywhere. The kids love attention and they buy into that whole phenomenon of becoming famous just by having your picture taken over and over.

ting in their darkened bedrooms listening to *Pornography* by The Cure."

POSTPUNK KIDS

Who Are They? Kids who have a vague cloud of angst hanging over them—or pretend they do—and relate to the gloomy, moody, yet humorous, sexually ambivalent songs of The Smiths, Morrissey, Sandie Shaw covering the Smiths, Nancy Sinatra covering Morrissey and more Smiths. When they need a break from The Smiths, they listen to Joy Division, New Order and Interpol. No one seems to understand them, the poor things. They are human and they need to be loved, just like everybody else does.

The Look: Black hair and pale skin; but they are sometimes too busy sulking to bother applying eye makeup (even the girls). The Postpunk Kids are stealth fashionistas and subsist on a diet of Raf Simons, Dior Homme, Rick Owens, Carpe Diem, Cloak, Ann

Continued

Demeulemeester, and Helmut Lang. Other staples include Smiths T-shirts, Joy Division tees fashioned into dresses, skull-motif tank tops, combat boots, and intense frowns. The more extreme of the species have taken to tattooing Smiths and Morrissey song titles on their bodies, i.e. "Handsome Devil" above a nipple or "Seasick, Yet Still Docked" across an entire thigh.

Pavlovian Response: Goosebumps when the opening guitar chord of "How Soon is Now?" is heard.

Diagnosis: Despite over a decade of gay visibility in the mainstream media, there are still legions of wan boys (and their sympathetic wan girlfriends) who consult the Oracle of Morrissey for answers about their murky sexual identities and feelings. When Moz finally brings them to the light at the end of the tunnel, they either give themselves over to a vapid life of sexual fulfillment or continue on the path of miserable

Continued

The MisShapes photos are not candid—the kids pose as if they're on a red carpet. These kids want to be famous and they're not antiestablishment by any means. It's like when Marilyn Manson wrote that song, "The Beautiful People," which was a commentary about the corrupt nature of fame, and later he ended up becoming what he was satirizing . . . and now it seems like he hates himself because of it."

Todd, a somewhat clueless member of Miss Guy's entourage, calls ahead to Thomas on his cell phone. "Hey, doll! I'm with Miss Guy and Michael Schmidt and we're coming over to MisShapes now!"

"Uhm, I'm aware," Thomas says, sounding annoyed to have had to take the call while working his post in front of the club. "The VIP area is being set up for you guys as we speak." Miss Guy, an androgynous rock performer who once fronted a band called The Toilet Boys, has been on the New York scene since the mid-'eighties when he lipsynched bubbly dance numbers at Boy Bar. Tonight he has just finished a one-person show at The Knitting Factory—a sort of hard-rock version of Ann-Margret's famous Las

Vegas act—and he is on his way to MisShapes to unwind with a group of friends. There is a feeling of parents making an unexpected appearance at a high school prom in the air.

"What do you mean, the kids in their early twenties listen to 'eighties music at this place?" Rafael—a raven-haired, alabaster-skinned New York club veteran—asks incredulously during the cab ride. "It's true!" Todd exclaims. "I've been to this club and they listen to the *same* songs I danced to when I was in high school in 1984!"

"That's ridiculous," Rafael snorts. "Don't they have anything *new* to listen to?"

"They do," Todd tells her. "But a lot of the new bands sound just like the old ones."

Besides Rafael, Todd, and Michael, Guy's entourage also includes Lauren Pine—who is attired in one of her famous corsets—and Astro, a die-hard clubber who has probably been out every single night since 1980. When they arrive at the club, Debbie Harry—sporting a new red hairdo—is lingering outside, talking to a group of friends. The young hipsters—who are standing around in outfits that were inspired by Harry's CBGB's punk rock days—don't seem to recognize her, but a few glance quizzically at Guy and company as they pull up to the ropes.

enlightenment (or split their time between both).

Advertising/Marketing Potential: None. Unless Morrissey decides to sell the lyrics "And if a double-decker bus/Crashes into us" to Mitsubishi.

The Door Bitch's Decree: "The sun shines out of the behinds of these eternally adorable mopers."

THE GAYS

Who Are They? Not to be confused with the sexually ambiguous boys who cling to their gal pals with an Oedipal fervor, or even the more homosexually confident hipsters, The Gays might be slightly older—over twenty five—and, ironically, more subdued in their look. There is a feeling that this species is taking a break from dancing shirtless at some jumbo techno palace and are slumming with the rocker kids at this "cute little place we read about in the gay section of *Time Out*."

Continued

Continued

The Look: Low-rise Diesel jeans with bulging baskets, tight T-shirts that display palsied attempts at irony ("Hooters Palm Beach"), tank tops, sleeveless shirts, sports mesh tops, terry cloth headbands, Izod polo tops, and Prada dancing shoes. Because this crew is so obsessed with having their underwear seen before the sun comes up, they may forgo the $2^{(x)}$ist contour pouch briefs for one night in exchange for a pair of "hipper" Ginch Gonch multi-colored star-print trunks.

Pavlovian Response: When "Filthy and Gorgeous" by the Scissor Sisters comes on, these boys get fuuunky!

Diagnosis: Not only can they dance circles around Gwen Stefani and Britney, the gays also serve a useful purpose here: they allow the more sexually indecisive hipsters an opportunity to break away from their college girlfriends and take a ride down the Hershey Highway. (Or, if their admirers belong to the postpunk species, another moment of anguished,

"Hello, gorgeous," Thomas says to Guy, giving him a big hug. Todd starts pulling on the sleeve of Thomas's striped Burberry shirt. "Doll, do you have any drink tickets?"

"Nope, no drink tickets. Instead, you'll just have to settle for free bottle service all night long . . . I'm sure you'll make do." Thomas escorts the group into the club and over to an area in a far corner where velvet ropes separate some white banquettes from the rest of the venue. A busboy is busy putting bottles of Southern Comfort and Absolut into ice buckets and arranging decanters of cranberry juice and tonic. "If you guys need anything else, please let me know," Thomas tells them. The group settles into the banquettes, reaching for bottles of booze and peering beyond the ropes at the skinny kids in the room by the bar who are hopping around like scrawny bunnies. The DJ upstairs, a twenty-one-year-old named Ryan, puts on "Spellbound" by Siouxsie and the Banshees. "See!? I told you!" Todd exclaims to Rafael as he reaches for a bottle of Absolut, pulls it out of the ice bucket, and fills more than half his cup with vodka. "And has anyone noticed that I'm the only one here with muscles and a tan?"

"Some of the kids here look like they have

CONFESSIONS FROM THE VELVET ROPES

scurvy," Lauren observes with almost motherly concern. "And why is everyone so skinny? They're, like, *really* skinny." She turns her corseted back to Todd. "Darling, could you tighten me up a few notches?" "Why are we roped off and separated from the young people?" Rafael says with a hint of self-conscious sarcasm in her voice. "Is this the *Logan's Run* corner?" she asks, referring to the science fiction film in which citizens of a futuristic society are extermi-nated on their thirtieth birthdays. "Honey, if this was the *Logan's Run* corner, we all would've been piles of ash before this club was even built," Todd says as he simultaneously takes a big gulp of his drink and adjusts the strap of his black $2^{(x)}$ist tank top while looking in the mir-ror. Michael grabs Todd by the arm, causing him to spit out his drink. "Come on, Dorian Gray, let's go check out what's going on upstairs."

When the pair ascends to the cramped dance floor, the crowd is dancing spastically to a song by Interpol. "Can't you see what you've done to my heart . . . and soul/It's just a wasteland now. . . ."

"Whatta these kids know about broken hearts and souls?" Todd says bitterly as a pogo-ing boy in a T-shirt printed with DESTROY above a swastika almost knocks his vodka and tonic

unfulfilled desire, followed by a five-A.M. crying session at home while listening to *Hatful of Hollow*.)

Advertising/Marketing Potential: Eternal. Homosexual anxiety will never, ever go out of style in advertising.

The Door Bitch's Decree: "Miss Thing, your hair looks *fierce*. Have a drink ticket."

GOTHS

Who Are They? Kids who are members of a widespread cult that, like punk, astonishes and amuses with its timeless resilience. With their affinity for death obses-sion, depression, and clove cig-arettes, the quaint goths—like Red Bull and vodka—are a must for any rock party . . . as long as there aren't too many of them. Their musical tastes tend to overlap with the '80s New Wavers and the post-punks, while the jury is still out on Marilyn Manson: goth God or Sad Sellout? It's not a good idea to mention the Columbine

Continued

incident around these kids—unless you want to be subjected to a tedious, clove smoke–saturated diatribe.

The Look: Lots of black (of course) and blood red dresses, sheer tops, skirts etc., gathered crinoline petticoats, corsets, black lipstick and heavy black eye makeup (a must for the girls and boys), tongue studs, crucifixes, black patent leather, oversized combat boots, platform boots, fishnet stockings, spiked dog collars, punk/goth T-shirts (Bauhaus/Peter Murphy, Siouxsie Sioux, Christian Death, The Faint), black blazers with black stovepipe pants on some of the less transgendered boys.

Pavlovian Response: "Bela Lugosi's Dead" by Bauhaus is still the goth "Stairway to Heaven."

Diagnosis: While not quite as stylistically inventive as their Japanese counterparts, the American goths get points for their steadfast commitment to outsider audacity and for their

Continued

out of his hand. "Excuuuuse me!" Todd bellows like a foghorn, but the boy is oblivious. Michael is already chatting up a guy wearing an open black leather vest with no shirt. A skinny black leather tie falls against his lean torso. "I'm gonna go outside and get some air," Todd tells Michael, who is too busy admiring the lean boy's cheekbones to hear him. Outside, Thomas is busy fending off the masses from the now-packed club. He faces the line of people that now trails several yards down the sidewalk. "Some of you are very cute, in fact, you're all really gorgeous," he announces in a loud voice. "But you're probably going to have to wait for an hour . . . and I don't want to hear any yelling and complaining."

Three zaftig Latina girls in tight skirts and tight blouses adorned with an abundance of sequined appliqués sigh in unison and form a huddle to try to figure out what to do with the rest of their evening. A pair of reed-thin girls in off-the-shoulder tees and heavy eyeliner squeeze past them and present themselves before Thomas. Thomas recognizes them as regulars and swiftly whisks them over to the hand stamp station before anyone waiting in line even notices. Todd sneaks up behind Thomas and wraps his arms around him. "You're all *really, really* gorgeous! Really you are!" he coos mockingly into Thomas's ear. "You're *so* sincere, Mr. Door Bitch."

"Larry Tee is over there, why don't you go say hi and reminisce about the days when you rode to clubs in a horse and buggy," Thomas says to him sardonically.

"Those were the days . . . Larry DJed with an old Victrola and Abe Lincoln and I did coke together in the backroom of the Gettysburg-a-Go-Go," Todd says with faux wistfulness before making his way over to Larry. "Hey Larry, love your shirt," Todd says, greeting him with a kiss on both cheeks. Larry is wearing a black, smock-like top that is bizarrely adorned with a sunglass-wearing sunburst, rendered in yellow sequins. Larry, a well-known DJ who hails originally from Atlanta, Georgia, famously came to New York in 1988 with his band, The Now Explosion, and a van load of performers including RuPaul—he later penned the song "Supermodel" for her. He's also a self-described trend observer.

"I love the outfits here, they're so retarded," he tells Todd. "These kids are so young, no one has ever told them how they should dress . . .

obsessive interests in art and literature. From Siouxsie Sioux's banana split lady to Anne Rice novels to *The Nightmare Before Christmas*, the goth zeitgeist keeps on ticking like the Doomsday Clock.

Advertising/Marketing Potential: Some. The gag of showing the disparity between goth teens and their intolerant parents pops up in cereal and cell phone commercials as well as forgettable movies.

The Door Bitch's Decree: "After they drop the nuclear bomb, all that will be left are cockroaches, Cher, and goths."

SELF-ENTITLED WHITE PEOPLE Who Are They? Men and women who went to good schools, have steady corporate jobs, and act like they own the streets of New York. It should be noted that a Self-Entitled White Person does not necessarily have to be Caucasian.

Continued

[85]

Continued

but I think Thomas does a great job of deciding who has made a sincere effort and who needs to be sent back to the drawing board."

"Why do you think the kids are doing the 'eighties all over again?" Todd says as he looks over and notices Thomas chatting amicably with Debbie Harry.

"The 'eighties is just a better palette to pick from. The bands looked cool then and the kids here are keyed into that . . . and this isn't the time to recycle baggy raver pants." Larry gazes at a boy in an Iggy Pop tee and tight black jeans as he speaks. "I need a pair of tight jeans . . . and I need to lose weight," he laments as he lifts up his smock to reveal a fur-covered paunch. "Plump DJs are *so* 'nineties, so Frankie Knuckles! Or pumped-up guys," he pokes Todd's right deltoid for emphasis, "that look is so not right anymore. Thin is in. I need to get a pair of skinny jeans . . . if I show up for DJ gigs looking like a chubby forty-five-year-old, my stock will go down!"

"Well, then I better go talk to Thomas about having the club install a liposuction station ASAP, doll. It wouldn't be a pretty sight to witness the Larry Tee stock market crash in the midst of all these au courant slivers of flesh."

[86]

When Thomas is done talking to Debbie, he motions Larry and Todd over to his post by the ropes. "Do you two legends want your photo taken by the MisShapes photographer?" Thomas asks them. "He's right inside by the bar, if you go back in now you'll be able to find him." Before Thomas has finished his sentence, Todd and Larry are through the door faster than you can say "beautiful people."

Advertising/Marketing Potential: Engraved in stone. After all, they're the status quo. They're also the ones who advertisers hawk "cool" lifestyles to. Doesn't seem to be working, though.

The Door Bitch's Decree: "Sorry guys, it's a private party tonight. Try coming back next week a little earlier, like at seven thirty, and maybe you'll get in."

5

You can't stop the music, nobody can stop the music.
　　　　　　　　—THE VILLAGE PEOPLE

For all the legendary, perfect parties that have been held throughout history, there are just as many disastrous, Titaniclike nights that, in some cases, are even more spectacular—or at least more memorable—than the smoothly-run soirees. The Marchesa Casati—Belle Époque-era It Girl and muse to designers John Galliano and Tom Ford—threw infamous parties at her Venice palazzo and her pink marble villa outside of Paris. Dramatic storms often plagued and ruined her extravagant events, such as the deluge that dumped on her notorious Bal du Noir—a celebration held in honor of her muscular, black servant's prowess in the bedroom. The dress code included mandatory blackface makeup, which streamed onto La Casati's marble floors after the guests were caught in the downpour.

There are also cinematic parties gone awry, such as New Year's Eve in *The Poseidon Adventure*, in which guests attempted to scale an inverted Christmas tree aboard a luxury liner that had turned belly-up in the middle of the ocean. Faye Dunaway at a cocktail party foiled by fire in *The Towering Inferno* was another pandemonium-packed party gone wrong. And then there are the near-cataclysmic episodes from New York City's clubland during the beginning of the twenty-first century. From complaining, combative neighbors to unruly crowds to horrendous club management—not to mention the requisite torrential rainstorm—Thomas has been in the thick of it to bring levelheaded, grace-under-pressure chaos control to parties gone out of bounds.

Far from the madding crowds of twenty-somethings with cartoonishly long bangs, "Queen Bitch" T-shirts, and prematurely compromised livers, Thomas is standing sentry in front of the Zegna store on Madison Avenue. The invite-only crowd of socialites, fashion editors, and celebrities are filing politely into the upscale store—known for its pricey Italian suits—sans the rock 'n' roll raucousness that is part and parcel of the Door Bitch's world. A phalanx of photographers is stationed inside and out, snapping photos of the arrivals. The guests are not the sort of crowd who would log onto blogs such as Gawker.com or Lastnightsparty.com the next day to look for photos of themselves (or, at least they would never admit it), because they are more likely to end up in the pages of the *New York Times* Style section, or *Vogue*.

The occasion is the opening of the Zegna store, and its launch is being hosted by actor Adrien Brody, who has modeled in ads for the Italian company. Dressed in a deep blue Zegna suit, Adrien arrives with his date Lauren DuPont—an heiress in the DuPont family—who is dressed in a pink minidress accessorized with a Chihuahua. Inside, Adrien is greeted by a member of the Zegna family. "Happy Birthday, Adrien," one says, giving the Oscar-winning actor a warm hug. Over the next few hours, more guests arrive—fashion editors, sports stars, supermodel Carol Alt, socialite Fabian Basabe— and Thomas dutifully checks them off the list while keeping his eyes turned away from the constant barrage of paparazzi camera flashes. After all the guests have arrived and a brief lull falls on this patch of Madison Avenue, a woman in her late fifties—her jet black hair pulled back into a ponytail—appears alone in front of the store. "I'm Adrien's mom," Sylvia Plachy, the Hungarian-born photographer, tells Thomas. He takes Sylvia by the hand and guides her through the mobbed ground floor of the store, up the stairs, and toward the VIP area where Adrien is holding court. Emilia, one of the publicists working the event, spots Thomas and walks over to greet Sylvia. "Sylvia, you're here!" Emilia says. "It's so great to see you. Adrien is right over there." As she's about to lead Sylvia to the other side of the room she turns to Thomas. "You should probably go downtown soon," she says. "I'll see you there in a little while."

As Thomas makes his way back through the crowd of Zegna advertising executives in expensive suits, and fashion-istas in expensive everything, his cell phone rings. It's Meg, an-other publicist who has helped plan this event and the upcoming after party—a private birthday bash for Adrien and his friends that will be held in the East Village. "How are things going up there?" she asks.

"Everything's fine, Meg. I just walked the birthday boy's mom in and the store is packed with well-behaved glitterati. Are you guys all set up down there?"

"Almost. I'm waiting for the DJ Stretch Armstrong to show up. When are you coming down? You should probably get set up with Zach at the door very soon."

"You got it Meg, see you in about fifteen."

Two minutes later Thomas is in a cab heading down to East First Street, to the private residence where the party will be held. He greets his friend Zach who will be helping him check in guests at the door of the party. "How was the store opening, and where's my gift bag, Santa Claus? I'm salivating for some of that Zegna swag," Zach jokes as he hands a clipboard with the guest list and a pair of headsets to Thomas.

"Sorry, I didn't get you a gift bag, but I'm chewing a piece of gum that Amy Sacco gave me—you want it?" Thomas pushes the gum out of his mouth slightly with his tongue.

"I don't want your semicelebrity sloppy seconds," Zach says with a grimace. "Hey, look—someone's early." Thomas and Zach both look up and a chic brunette, wearing a shearling jacket and carrying a Dior bag, is walking toward the door. "Hi, how are you?" Thomas says politely. "Can I have your last name, please?"

"Greece," she tells him. Zach starts flipping through his copy of the list. "I'm sorry, how do you spell that?"

"It's Greece, like the country," she says demurely. Thomas and Zach flip back and forth through the pages of their lists when Thomas suddenly spots a "Princess Olga of Greece" on it. "Oh, here you are," Thomas says, wondering if he should kneel, curtsy, or merely maintain his usual nonchalant demeanor. Zach opens the door for her and Thomas radios Meg on his headset. "We've got an early arrival, Meg, I hope the champagne is already on ice. Princess Olga from Greece just walked in."

"I never would have realized she was a princess," Zach says. "She must have left her tiara in her chariot." Next to arrive is Fabian Basabe. Although he showed up stag for the Zegna event, the notorious It Boy now has three dates in tow: George Bush's niece, Lauren Bush, Lauren's publicist, and Amanda Hearst. Over the next thirty minutes, guests continue to arrive in droves, pulling up in limos, Lincoln town cars, and cabs. The A-to-C-list roster includes: M. Night Shyamalan, the director, Moby, Amy Sacco, Rena Sindi, the author, Ann Dexter Jones, editors from *Conde Nast Traveler,* the requisite gaggle of models, a couple of track-suited friends of the DJ. By midnight the party is going full throttle and guests are cavorting in the courtyard to Stretch Armstrong's hip-hop mix. "Thomas, get a load of this number," Zach says in a low voice, as a tall man in his late fifties, dressed in sweatpants and a wrinkled flannel shirt strides quickly toward the door. Thomas looks him up and down coolly. "Uuuhm . . . are you on the list?"

"Do you know who I am?" the man says boldly. *Oh boy, we've got a real live one here,* Thomas thinks. Thomas decides to err on the side of politeness. After all, he could be some strung-out Hollywood producer or the owner of a modeling agency. He could be Fabian Basabe's long-lost uncle. "Well . . . you *do* look kind of familiar," Thomas says carefully. "Are you a friend of Adrien's?"

"I'm Randy Jones. I was the cowboy in The Village People." Zach tries to stifle a laugh and starts coughing. Randy holds up his watch and starts tapping it and says in an annoyed voice, "It's midnight. If you don't turn the music down, I'm going to call the police."

"I'm sorry sir, but I'm not in charge of the music . . . I could talk to one of my colleagues and—"

"I want to speak to the person in charge now," Randy interrupts. Thomas leaves him with Zach, steps inside the door, and radios Meg. "There's a rather interesting neighbor out here complaining about the noise from the party," he informs her.

"Oh, we were warned about the neighbors whose buildings face the courtyard. Apparently they complain all the time. Just invite them in and offer them a drink."

"Meg, it's no ordinary neighbor . . . it's the guy who used to play the cowboy in the Village People. And he's angry. I don't think he's exactly a sparkling addition to this soiree."

"The cowboy from the Village People?! Are you kidding?

Well, do your best to humor him. I'll ask Emilia to come out and talk to him." Meg clicks off and Thomas steps back outside. "Randy, would you like to come inside and have a glass of champagne?" Thomas has now put on his impending-damage-control persona. Emilia appears at the door with a plastic smile on her face. "Hello there . . . we'd love to have you as a guest at our party. Come in, have a drink and mingle." She glances at his sweatpants and wrinkled shirt and her smile tightens. "I do *not* want a drink, I want the music turned down *now!*" Randy says. "I live in the building behind your courtyard and the music is annoying me and my neighbors. It's Tuesday night—people have to get up and go to work and their kids have to go to school!"

"I'm terribly sorry, I'll tell the DJ to turn down the music," Emilia says and disappears back inside the house. Seemingly placated, Randy turns around and leaves without saying another word. "Didn't The Village People once make a movie called *Can't Stop the Music?*" Thomas says to Zach. "Ironic, no?"

About ten minutes later the police arrive, barge into the party, and ask Emilia to tell the DJ to turn down the music. "Okay, everything should be all right now," Meg radios in to Thomas. But five minutes later, the cross cowboy is back. "Oh lord, the party pooper is back," Zach mutters under his breath.

"We can still hear the music," Randy says with extreme annoyance. Fed up, Thomas decides to just give him a little handling. "Okay, okay, we'll turn the music down, Randy. Sorry about that." Randy storms off. "Maybe if we asked Stretch to

put on a remix of 'YMCA,' the cowboy will leave us alone?"
Thomas wonders aloud. He then radios Meg and asks if she can
have the music turned down further. Meg answers by radioing
Thomas and Zach simultaneously. "Okay, Thomas . . . Zach,
can you come back here and help me close the doors to the
courtyard? Maybe that will muffle some of the sound coming
from the speakers inside." Zach disappears into the house, leaving Thomas behind to welcome in a few late arrivals. A few
minutes later, Zach calls him on his headset. "Thomas . . . oh
my god! They are throwing *eggs* into the courtyard! Eggs! Can
you believe it?!"

"Are you joking?!" Thomas asks. "This is insane, those
neighbors are ridiculous! Are the guests okay?"

"Thomas, it's like a biblical plague! Dozens of eggs are rain-
ing down on the courtyard!!" *This is* not *a good development,*
Thomas is thinking. As he's imagining egg yolk sliding down
Adrien's formidable nose, Meg's voice comes booming through
Thomas's headset. "Oh my god, Thomas, Lauren Bush just got
hit with an egg and she's trying to leave!" Meg sounds slightly
hysterical. "She's on her way out to you and I'm right behind
her with club soda and a towel!" As Thomas turns around to
see if Lauren is on her way—*wham!*—the Bush bombshell
slams right into him, looking extremely flustered. Towel-
bearing Meg emerges from the house. "An egg hit Lauren's
shoe, but I think she's alright otherwise," Meg says as she follows Lauren into the street. Trailing behind her are Lauren's
publicist, Fabian, and Amanda Hearst.

"I'm so sorry this happened," Meg says when she catches up with Lauren. "Is there anything I can do?" Thomas notices that Lauren is wearing a killer pair of black stilettos—most likely Gucci—but he can't make out signs of an egg attack on her expensive footwear. When Lauren realizes the damage isn't as bad as she thought, she and her entourage return to the party. As Zach reappears at the door, the police are back again to reinvestigate the music problem.

"I can't wait to go home and burn all my Village People records," Thomas quips. "That is, if I owned any."

For the past seven months, Thomas has worked the doors of an upscale hip-hop party at Coral Room. Each week, men in tailored suits or expensive hip-hop wear, and women, for whom bling-bling is more a religion than an accessory concept, pony up to the ropes and order two-hundred-plus-dollar bottles of alcohol once inside the coral-textured walls of the club. The latest hip-hop, R & B, and disco classics are spun by DJ Reach, who also mans the turntables on *The Carson Daly Show*. Thomas doesn't even glance at the mermaid go-go girls swimming around in the forty-foot long, nine-thousand-gallon fish tank behind the bar as he rushes toward the club's main lounge. He surveys the packed, sea foam green–painted room, where waitresses struggle to pass through the crowd so they can deliver bottles of vodka and rum to the suited men and short-skirted girls seated together at tables.

"Chris, we've got a real situation out there," Thomas says to the club's general manager and co-owner, who is standing near the entrance to the lounge with Jed and Alex, two promoters for the club. "There's a mob of people who are on the guest list, clamoring to get in." Even though it is a chilly November evening, beads of sweat have formed on Thomas's forehead. "Well, we obviously can't let any more people in," Chris says as he makes an agitated gesture toward the lounge. "People are swinging from the rafters in here! Tell them we're sorry, but the list is closed for the night." *Oh great,* Thomas thinks, *I'm going to tell two hundred people—who all think they're mega-important—that Saturday night's hottest party is closed to them tonight.*

Over the past few months the party's popularity has gained momentum—with appearances by such A-listers as Paris and Nicky Hilton, Tyson Beckford, and Mark Ronson—and as a result, Thomas and the security team have been asked to tighten up the door policy: men who arrive in bargain-basement hip-hop wear, casual athletic clothing, and baseball caps are turned away. The corporate, industry vibe of the clientele—moneyed, ostentatious, connected—represents one of the phenomena that many members of New York's demimonde blame for the decline of the city's once-anarchic nightlife. The filthy lucre exhibitionism of bottle service is anathema to legions of rocker kids and style rebels who scoff at the idea of impressing rivals with an exorbitant bar tab. Thomas is pretty much over the scene at Coral Room, although one of the things that keeps him there—besides rent money—is the camaraderie he has with the club's staff.

"What's the story, Thomas my man?" Herb, the club's head of security, asks Thomas as he returns to his station at the ropes. Herb, a muscular, black, off-duty police officer, has been moonlighting as a club security guard for a number of years and knows how to work all different types of nightlife crowds.

"They're full to capacity in there," Thomas reports. "We can't let anyone else in." Thomas looks out at the mob scene—about two hundred people are waiting in line behind a long velvet rope, while at least another fifty are gathered around the front of 'the box,' ten people deep in a semicircle. The crowd is literally closing in on them and has slowly pushed the ropes toward the door, causing 'the box,' where Thomas and Herb are standing, to shrink in size. *This crowd could definitely get violent,* Thomas thinks to himself. "Oh my lord, this is out of control!" exclaims Heather, the club's bottle hostess, who has come outside to survey the scene and is now standing next to Thomas. The petite brunette, dressed in black pants, black tee, and black shoes, spends the rest of her week working in art sales. "It's so crowded inside, the waitresses can't even get through the crowd to bring bottles to the tables!" she tells Thomas. A group of model-like girls at the front of the line wave at Thomas. "Hello, could you please stop ignoring us? We're on the guest list!" Thomas walks over to them thinking: *they look great; I would totally want them in this party.* "I'm really sorry girls, you look gorgeous, but the club is full and we can't let anyone else in tonight."

"What are you talking about? We're on the guest list."

"I know you are, but I still can't let anyone else in."

"But we're on the guest list." *Okay, this is really just not sinking in,* Thomas thinks when he suddenly feels Herb's hand on his shoulder. "Thomas, we need to do this, we need to take control of the situation," Herb tells him. "This is how it's gonna go—we're literally going to close the doors to the club and lock them. Some of us will be locked outside and the rest of the security team will be inside. If this situation cools down in about an hour, we'll reopen the doors and try to let more people in . . . but, basically, it's exits only now." Herb then turns to one of the other security guards and says loudly, "Hey, go inside and get Shaka. We're gonna do this old school." *Wow, Shaka,* Thomas thinks. *They're bringing in the big guns.*

A few moments later, the door to the club flies open and Shaka, a six-foot-nine, hulking presence, emerges. Unlike the other guards who are wearing dark blazers, Shaka is wearing a black leather jacket that looks like it's straight out of *The Matrix.* The outsized flashlight he's carrying resembles a laser weapon, poised for destruction. The crowd in front of the ropes instinctively moves back a few steps. "Okay boys, let's do this," Shaka says in a booming voice. Herb and Shaka push the doors shut and lock them. This happens so quickly, Heather doesn't have a chance to go back into the club. "Hey, wait, I'm still out here," she cries, but her plea falls on deaf ears. Herb and Shaka have already moved outside the ropes and begin walking menacingly through the crowd like storm troopers. Heather looks at Thomas, wide-eyed. "Oh my god, we're going to die out here," she says slowly. Heather makes a vain attempt to open the exit door, but it only opens from the inside. Thomas puts his arm around her and whispers in her ear, "Don't panic. They can smell fear."

Shaka advances toward the line of people and a group of girls retreat toward the wall of the club. He gathers up the velvet ropes and stanchions that form the waiting area and sweeps them away in his powerful arms. The crowd of people who were in line begins to slowly disperse. More people press against the ropes of the box and shout at Thomas.

"I'm friends with Paris Hilton and I'm meeting her here tonight, you have to let me in!"

"Please let us in, our friends are waiting for us inside!"

"The club is closed? What the fuck are you talking about? Don't you know who I am?"

"Please, I just want to run in and use the bathroom—I have a bladder problem!"

"I was just in there and I left my Chanel bag behind the DJ booth!" Others pull out their cell phones and begin calling people they know who are inside the club. Thomas stands away from them, near the locked doors, trying to look cool and detached. What the hell will it take for them to get it? As he begins fantasizing about nightclubs on wheels that can be driven away like trailers, he hears Shaka's deep voice resonating through the crowd. "I don't care if you're friends with Paris and Nicky Hilton—they are not here. Go home now! We are calling the police to help us disperse the crowd!"

Suddenly, Thomas feels the exit door behind him swing open and bump him in the back. He and Heather turn around and see a man emerge with a cell phone clamped urgently to the side of his head, as if it were a mini life support system. "I'm outside now," he yells through the phone. "Where the hell are you, man?" Thomas touches his shoulder and begins to close the door on him. "Go back inside!" he barks. "Your friends are not getting in."

"But I'm—," the man begins to protest.

"Shut up and go back inside," Thomas orders before the man has a chance to finish his sentence.

Forty-five minutes pass and the doors remain locked. Despite the fact that the shut-out party people were told they would not get into the club, no way, no how, at least twenty people have remained waiting in front of the club, chain smoking and chain cell phoning. *What the hell kind of person would stand in front of a locked club after they've been told repeatedly to go home?* Thomas wonders to himself. *There are so many clubs in this city, can't they just go somewhere else? Have they no dignity?* A few moments later, Herb—who has been regaling Thomas, Shaka, and Heather with tales from police blotters past—decides that it's now okay to unlock the doors and reopen the club. Apparently, enough people have exited at this point and there is now

breathing room inside. So sure enough, the twenty diehards are
allowed into the club, following Heather in as she leads them
to tables and gives them the rundown of the bottle procedure.
The mermaid go-go swimmers in the enormous fish tank continue to cavort with schools of silver fish, oblivious to the evening's earlier crowd control dilemma. Outside, Shaka gives
Thomas a good-natured slap on the back, nearly knocking the
husky doorman over. "You kept your cool, my man," Shaka ex-
alts him. "Sometimes these situations can get pretty rough,
you know what I'm sayin'?"

"Oh, I wasn't worried," Thomas lies, relieved that the
whole ordeal is past. "I've been in the trenches before and I
know I'll be in them again." Shaka goes back inside and
Thomas spends the rest of the night imagining a worst-case
scenario. *Suppose I had been shot tonight at the door, just because I
was doing my job by not letting anyone else in?* he asks himself.
*Would there be a public outcry, like when a police officer is gunned
down? Would I become a nightlife martyr? Would my body be laid out
in a crisp, black Cloak designer suit in front of the giant fish tank?*

"We are gathered here today to pay tribute to our dearly,
departed Door Bitch . . . who died in the line of duty, battling
the scourges of clubland . . . he fought and vanquished the
Paris Hilton friends who aren't really Paris Hilton friends, the
badly dressed, the boorish, the banal. Thomas Onorato gave his
life so you, dear clubgoer, would not have to spend the night
sitting in an overcrowded banquette next to someone who buys
their Dolce and Gabbana—last season's Dolce and Gabbana,

no less—at outlet stores in Jersey—so you, dear nightclubber, can feel special spending three hundred dollars on a bottle of vodka while some poor slob is downing draught beer at a doorman-less dive in another borough. Thomas Onorato died for the sins of the *real* Paris Hilton friends, the sins of hip-hop royalty, the keepers of the Bling and everything fly, the sins of the Versace fragrance–anointed elitist masses . . . The Chosen People who are always on the Guest List. Let us pray, dear bottle service devotees, to the Fathers—Diddy, Jay-Z, 50 Cent, The Game, etcetera—their bitches, and the Holy Ghost of Tupac, Amen."

"Oh no, it's ruined!" Thomas moans as he holds up the limited edition Andy Warhol T-shirt he wore the night before. The shirt—which features a print of the invitation Warhol designed in 1983 for the New York club Area—is stained with black eye makeup, blue ink, and unidentifiable New York City grime. The word "Art," which Warhol had rendered as appearing in fractured glass, is barely legible; the address of the long-lost club printed below it is completely blotted out. Thomas plunges the shirt into a sink full of warm water and Woolite—his third attempt to wash out the stains—as his mind drifts back to the horror of last night . . .

"Jesús H. Christ, I can barely read this damn guest list!" Thomas exclaims as he lifts a soggy page up from the clipboard he is holding. He is standing in the pouring rain in front of

Club Shelter on West Thirty-ninth Street with Zach and Autumn. "And the night has only begun!" The event is the Motherfucker Labor Day Weekend Party, and the headlining band that Mofo promoter Justine D. has booked for the party is The Rapture—a Brooklyn rock quartet whose spectrum of influences runs the gamut from Gang of Four to Bowie to deep Chicago house. The band had arrived three hours earlier, but because the soundman that had been booked was MIA, a sound check has not taken place. This is the least of the night's problems: Despite the fact that the club was booked for the Mofo party exclusively, the owners of Shelter decided at the last minute to lease out the basement to a hip-hop party. So, outside of the venue lined up toward Sixth Avenue are the polymorphously perverse Mofo regulars and on the other side, a line of frequently homophobic hip-hoppers. "This is a recipe for disaster!" Zach says to Thomas as he struggles to keep his guest list dry by holding it against his chest. "It's like inviting Leni Riefenstahl to a bar mitzvah!"

Thomas surveys the long line—which is wrapped around the block and continuing on to Thirty-eighth Street—of rocker kids and hipsters waiting in the torrential rain. A cavalcade of mushy hairdos, wilted mohawks, rivers of melted makeup, sloshy, slouchy suede boots, rock tees, and white, Victorian-style blouses drenched to the point of transparency—in fact, many of the girls look like they have entered a New Romantic revival wet T-shirt contest. And to make matters worse for them, the club management has combined the guest list, the will-call, and general admission lines into one, making the check-in process for Thomas, Zach, and Autumn an organizational disaster. "Can this get any worse?" Thomas asks Zach with exasperation, as he continues flipping through the sopping pages of his guest list.

"Whooa! Look at all the fucking homos!" Thomas hears someone yell and he looks down the long line. Walking past the lineup is a gang of men who are obviously arriving for the hip-hop party, shoving a couple of glam rock–looking boys and yelling as they move down the sidewalk. "I've never seen so many gay-ass bitches in my life!"

"Oh . . . my . . . lord," Thomas says in a panicked tone. "This is *so* not cool!" He makes an appeal to one of the bouncers to maintain order. "These kids aren't used to this kind of situation, they're like bunny rabbits—if you scare them away they won't come back. Could you please try to keep things under control?" The bouncer ignores him and fixes his gaze on four boys in skinny jeans and black sleeveless band shirts who have circumvented the line and are standing next to Thomas. "Oh, hey guys," Thomas greets them. "I'm so sorry about this, I know you're on the list, let me just get you in now—" The bouncer steps toward them and starts screaming. "Get to the end of the fucking line or go home! We don't care if you're on the guest list—it's all one line tonight!"

"Uhm, could you please not speak to our guests like that?" Thomas admonishes him. "You're really out of order." Veins bulge in the bouncer's neck, but before he has a chance to respond, another bouncer pulls him away for what looks like a miniconference.

"I really can't handle all this 'roid rage," Autumn says with disgust. "If I wanted this kind of bullshit, I would have stayed home and watched the International Wrestling Federation match on HBO." While the bouncers are distracted, Thomas walks up and down the sidewalk until he finds a few waiting press and industry people, quickly yanks them out of the line, and shuttles them into the club and through the narrow hallway where a cashier is stationed.

"Here's a bunch of drink tickets guys, sorry for all the chaos." When Thomas walks out of the club and back out into the rain, he witnesses another unexpected development in the night's already disastrous proceedings. The belligerent bouncers have begun erecting barricades up and down the length of the sidewalk, making it virtually impossible for anyone to walk down the street and over to the entrance of the club. Their only recourse is to get in the back of the line. "Good lord, how am I going to get the VIPs in through that blockade? This is like trying to throw a party in a prison camp!" Thomas wails to Zach. Just then, he spots a cherubic blonde woman in a white dress and her androgynous companion attempting to squeeze past the barricades and up to the front of the line. As they get closer, Thomas can see that it's Debbie Harry and Miss Guy. As he starts to make a move, the bouncer starts screaming bloody murder at them. "Can't you see that there's a fucking line?! Get your asses back there!" Thomas spins around, straining to keep his cool, and says to the bouncer, "Try to be as calm as you can, I know that is really hard . . . but listen to me. That's Debbie Harry and she cannot be made to wait."

"Who the hell is Debbie Harry?" the benighted bouncer asks. Thomas manages to maintain his calm demeanor. "She's the lead singer of Blondie, okay? Blondie. Surely you've heard of them." A dim flicker of recognition passes across the bouncer's face—as if he is straining to recall the lyrics to "The Tide is High"—and he grabs the barricade and moves it over slightly, allowing Debbie and Guy to pass through. Debbie is silent, with an annoyed and slightly scared look on her face. Thomas knows she's not the hugest fan of crowds, and when he spots another bouncer who is standing solidly in front of the door, with a grazing cow look on his face, he shouts, "VIPs COMING THROUGH!" The bouncer moves aside with a startled look on his face.

Meanwhile, inside the club, The Rapture has just begun their set. As they begin plowing through "House of Jealous Lovers," Justine D.—who is standing in the DJ booth with Michael T.—notices a few people in the crowd grimacing. The disappointed frowns escalate into a wave effect as the entire room seems to emanate dissatisfaction. "Oh god, they sound like they're playing inside a tin can at the bottom of a lake!" Justine moans. "A lot of people came here tonight specifically to see them play!"

After the band finishes the song, the lead singer—Luke

Jenner—speaks apologetically into the mike. "Thanks for coming out in this typhoonlike weather. . . . We're having some sound problems but we're trying to make the best of it." As they launch into their next song, the crowd—a good portion of which are Rapture fans—remains civil, and a few people in the back begin dancing ecstatically, despite the still-muddy sound.

Back outside in the pouring rain, Thomas, Zach, and Autumn look up from the drenched pages of their guest lists and see several police cars pull up to the front of the club. People from the hip-hop party have begun spilling out into the street and several policemen get out of their cars and walk through the entrance to the basement. "Oh lord, what the hell is going on now?" Thomas says to Zach. One of the bouncers turns to him and says, "There was a shooting in the basement."

"Of course there was," Autumn says, rolling her eyes. "But how can I think about gang violence right now when my new shoes are ruined!" A few moments later, the police emerge from the club with several men in handcuffs and one of the officers approaches Thomas. "Listen, we're closing this block off and shutting down the street," he informs him and before Thomas has a chance to ask any questions, the officer is ordering the other policemen to park their cars and erect barricades on either end of the street.

"Good lord, how are the rest of our guests supposed to get to our party?!" Zach exclaims. "This is ridiculous! And I can't even read this guest list anymore!"

"Is it really necessary for them to shut down the damn street?" Autumn asks as she removes one of her stilettos and shakes the water out of it.

"They're probably worried about gang retaliation or something," Thomas says distractedly, as he strains to look down the length of the still impossibly long line. "Oh no! Michael Musto, Joey Arias, Chi Chi Valenti, and Johnny Dynell are all at the back of the line!" Thomas shouts and then turns to the nearest bouncer. "You really need to open the barricade for a minute . . . I need to get in a very important nightlife journalist and three nightlife legends before they get soaked!"

"Everyone thinks they're a VIP in this town," the bouncer replies gruffly and reluctantly slides the barricade back.

"Darling!" Chi Chi, clad in a black velvet cape, greets Thomas. She's wielding a black umbrella with lace trim and an unflappable, die-hard attitude. "I love your makeup—you look like a goth raccoon!"

"Thank you so much for coming," Thomas tells her as he shuttles the group hastily into the club. It's now past two A.M. and The Rapture has finished their set. All four members are standing out on the wet, crowded sidewalk next to Thomas with forlorn expressions on their faces. "The sound situation was a disaster," Luke says. "We just want to load our stuff up and go back to Brooklyn. A friend of ours is on his way with his van to pick us and our equipment up."

"I'm really sorry about this, guys," Thomas tells them. "We really appreciate you coming out to the party and playing."

The band begins pulling out amps, synthesizers, and other equipment, and places them under the almost nonexistent overhang in front of the club in a desperate attempt to keep everything dry. "There's a lot of police drama going on out here," Thomas continues. "And they're not letting any cars onto the block. Let me see if there's a way we can convince the police sergeant to let the van through." Thomas runs over to the sergeant, brings him over to Luke and introduces them. After much haggling, the sergeant agrees to let the van through. Luke runs to the end of the block to wait for the van and explain the situation to his friend who is driving it. Thomas and Zach hold umbrellas over the equipment while Autumn tries her best to let more people in who have been waiting in the rain for over an hour. "This is like boot camp!" she yells at Thomas as she lifts the rope for a drenched couple who are holding a copy of the *New York Post* over their heads to keep dry. A few minutes later Luke comes running back to the door. "That police officer changed his mind—now they won't let the van through!"

"Fascists!" Zach scowls.

"That sergeant was pissing me off so much, I wanted to punch him in the face," Luke says, soaked and frustrated. He then looks back down the block and sees that, inexplicably, the cops have opened the barricades and let the van through.

"Thank god for small miracles," Autumn says, and Thomas and Zach begin helping the band load their equipment when the van pulls up to the front of the club.

At two-thirty the bouncers make a startling announcement.
"We gotta close the doors of the club, the police don't want us
to let anyone else in."

"What!?" Thomas shouts. "But there are still two hundred
people out here for our party, and they've been waiting in the
rain for a goddamn hour! We never close the door to this party
until three-thirty!"

"Look buddy, I don't make the rules, I just enforce them,"
the bouncer tells him. As Thomas, Autumn, and Zach begin
breaking the news to the crowd of soaked and pissed-off party
hopefuls, the bouncers advise them to go inside the club, "if
you wanna get paid before the night is over." Defeated, the trio
complies and enter Shelter soaked, grimy, and exhausted.
"Ugh! Look at my Area T-shirt!" Thomas whines. "It's completely ruined, and I'll never be able to get another one!"
Johnny T., one of the promoters of Mofo, greets them with an
agonized look on his face. "How did it go out there?" he asks
the disheveled threesome. He glances at the disintegrating
guest lists and frowns. "Are you going to be able to tally those
up?" he asks worriedly. The names on the guest lists have been
partly generated by contracted promoters, guest hosts, and
DJs, and each one receives payment based on how many of
their guests actually attended the party. Even though many of
these guests have paid reduced admission prices, they generate
income for the Mofo team by boosting drinks sales while also
bringing a specific vibe to the party, bolstering its reputation
as a cutting-edge event. "We're just going to have to try our

best in adding these up," Thomas groans, as a chunk of wet, inky paper falls from his clipboard and lands on one of his damp, pointy boots. "We'll have to do a lot of it by memory."

"How are things going in here?" Autumn asks Johnny.

"Well, the band sounded like they were playing inside an oil drum and the bar upstairs ran out of ice, cups, and vodka at two A.M.," Johnny says wearily.

"Jesus Christ!" Thomas exclaims. "What is this—the former Soviet Union?"

Zach collapses onto the floor near a bank of cash registers and makes a vain attempt to separate the wet tissue paperlike pages of his list as Thomas and Autumn join him.

At four A.M., after an hour of putting their waterlogged heads together and calculating the guest list totals, the door team heads upstairs to visit Michael T. in the DJ booth. People on the packed dance floor—who seem to have recovered from The Rapture's sound snafu—are shaking their groove things to "Suffragette City" by David Bowie. According to the contract Mofo has with Shelter, the party still has another hour to go. Justine D. walks into the booth and greets Thomas with a look of consternation on her face. "Those fucking bouncers just shut off the sound system downstairs and told David his DJ set was over," she announces. "And they've closed down the room, even though both our floors are supposed to stay open till five!"

"Oh god, this place really sucks," Thomas says. He looks across the room and notices that the management has turned off the colored-gel lights and have turned up the glaring, white lights in an effort to get people to leave. "We can never do an-other party here! This is so unprofessional!" As Thomas is fin-ishing his words, he notices one of the oversized bouncers making his way over to the DJ booth. "Oh shit, here comes trouble!"

"Okay guys, you need to stop the music—NOW," the bouncer announces with a threatening tone as he enters the DJ booth. "The police are outside, and if you don't turn off the music and send everyone home, they're gonna rush in here, shut down the party, and start making arrests." Thomas looks over at Michael T. and notices that he's seething but is making no move to turn off the soundboard. "That is total bullshit," Justine tells the bouncer. "We are not doing anything illegal. The bars stopped serving alcohol at four—that is, the bars that didn't run out of booze at two. Our contract states our party goes until five. And it will." The bouncer ignores her and looks over in Michael's direction. "Yo, did you hear me?" the bouncer yells at him as he starts lurching toward the soundboard. "I said turn off the fucking music!" Michael ignores him, picks up a microphone, and starts shouting over "Don't Change" by INXS. "The fascists who run this club are trying to shut down our party!" he informs the packed dance floor. "Are we going to let them do that?" Roars of "NO!" and "Fuck that shit!" rise up from the dance floor. The bouncer, looking like he could eat glass, starts rushing toward Michael. Justine, who is a svelte five feet eight, places herself between the beefy six-foot-four bouncer and Michael, raising her hand defiantly. "Uh-uh, no way—you are NOT shutting off the sound. This party goes till five fucking A.M.!" she yells up at him. "YOU CAN'T STOP THE MUSIC!" The INXS song ends and, because Michael is preoccupied with shouting through the mike, the music has stopped. The Mofo revelers stand on the dance floor, looking up at Michael, Justine, and the bouncer, and continue booing and yelling obscenities. Michael throws down the mike, presses a button on the console, turns up the volume and "Transmission" by Joy Division blasts through the speakers.

"Dance, dance, dance, dance, dance to the radio!" Ian Curtis's ghostly voice booms across the room and the crowd launches into fits of spastic dancing, as if a doom rock version of *Footloose* has spontaneously erupted. Thomas looks down at the sea of writhing bodies on the dance floor, which is now obnoxiously lit with daylight-bright lights. In the middle of the room he notices Carlos D.—the bass player from the post-punk-inspired band Interpol—dancing very dramatically. Clad in a black, mod-style suit and combat boots, with his hair gelled over to one side in a rigid sweep, he resembles an escapee from the Manchester institute for gloomy-chic rockers. The energy from the crowd seems to momentarily stun the advancing bouncer and he backs away slightly from Justine. "If I don't get to play 'Love Hangover' by Diana Ross," Michael T. says to Thomas of his traditional end-of-the-night last song, "I will be fucking *furious!*" When "Transmission" begins to wind down to its measured drum beats, Michael decides it's Diana Ross time. As "Love Hangover" begins priming itself up,

Michael turns to Thomas and says, "I'm going down there to dance—I'm not going to let these Shelter assholes ruin *my* party!" Thomas high-fives him. "Okay, I'll stay here and make sure Justine is okay." Diana Ross's sublime, syrupy voice begins to slowly pour itself over the room. "If there's a cure for this . . ." Michael joins the hundreds of people who have begun swaying ritualistically to the song's opening. Back in the DJ booth, Johnny T. has appeared with a frantic look on his face. "Thomas, the owners are really getting on my case, we have to turn off the music."

"But it's the last song, it's our tradition," Thomas tells him. "Michael will be crushed." "I don't wanna get . . . oooo-verrrr . . ." As the song lunges excitedly toward its peak, Johnny abruptly slides a lever down on the sound board bringing Miss Ross to a dead, silent halt. A collective groan rises from the crowd and, as if on cue, a large bouncer emerges from each of the four entrances around the dance floor and all of them begin screaming at the top of their lungs. "Get your fucking shit and get the fuck out of here now!" Indignantly, people begin moving toward the exit as the bouncers continue yelling and following them from behind in an intimidating manner. Michael races up to the DJ booth, and when he sees Johnny standing in front of the soundboard, he starts yelling hysterically. "What the fuck did you do?! You *know* that's always the last song of the night!"

"I'm really sorry Michael," Johnny says meekly. "I had to shut it off, the security staff was all over my ass."

"By turning off that song, you have put a *stake* through my *heart!*" Michael screams at him. "Ending that song before it was over was a terrible symbolic gesture . . . we've now lost something from this party that we will never get back!" Johnny slinks out of the DJ booth and Michael walks over to the microphone he threw on the floor earlier. He picks it up, pushes the sound lever back to its original position, and begins channeling his rage through the club's speakers as the bouncers continue herding the crowd toward the exits. "The people who run this club are FASCISTS! This is why clubs in New York SUCK! The owners of this club can go FUCK themselves!"

Meanwhile, on the dance floor Justine is fighting her own battle. "You fucking bouncers can't treat people this way! This is why I hate this fucking nightlife industry . . . it's because of people like you!" One of the bouncers makes a move for her. "Get the fuck away from me, don't you *dare* put your hands on me!!" The bouncer gives her a dirty look, shrugs, and continues herding the discontented party animals out the door. When Carlos D. passes by Justine during the mass exodus he winks at her and says, "I didn't know you had that in you!" Thomas makes his way over to her as well. "Are you okay, darling?" When they walk back outside they find David Pianka, the other DJ for the party, standing next to a pile of crates filled with records on the sidewalk. "Those assholes took all my stuff out of the DJ booth and dumped it out here in the rain!" he shouts. Luckily the rain has slowed to a mere drizzle and Thomas and David are able to load his stuff into a cab with a

minimum of damage. The cops and the cop cars and the barricades and the hip-hoppers are now gone and Thomas is wondering if he hallucinated that whole episode during his
deluged door duty. "We've thrown some amazing and
smoothly run parties," Thomas says sullenly to Justine as he
rubs at some of the splotches on his T-shirt. "Tonight—to put
it mildly—was not one of them." After Thomas kisses Justine
goodnight, he hops into a cab and stops at an all-night diner
near his building for a giant order of take-out French fries. The
second he walks in the door of his apartment he wolfs them
down while standing up in his kitchen. He collapses into bed
still dressed, the grimy Warhol tee clinging to his torso like a
slowly drying layer of papier-mâché.

6 .

The world is full of crashing bores.
—MORRISSEY

An attractive young Asian woman, wearing a slinky, black
halter dress, is standing in front of Thomas outside a guest
list–only party at a club called Plaid. "Your name?" Thomas
asks her. He peers at her over the top of a pair of black-rimmed
spectacles, which, along with his three-day beard, makes him
look like Edna from *The Incredibles* cross-bred with Russell
Crowe. "I'm Bai Ling," the woman announces confidently.
Thomas looks her up and down without consulting the guest
list. "Um, no you're not," he says with annoyance. "I know who
you are—you're a teller at my bank in Chinatown."

Uninvited liars. Star stalkers. Troublemakers. The phenomenon of persistent party crashers and boozy bores goes back at
least as far as the days when the Vikings crashed Christian
clambakes—where they proceeded to rape, pillage, and drink
for free. Several centuries later, when men attired in polyester
suits tried to crash Bianca Jagger's birthday party at Studio 54,

strict measures to keep out the unwanted had been adopted: intimidating velvet ropes, large bouncers, self-esteem crushing VIP lists, and withering sarcasm from doormen. These measures are still in use today. "If I don't know you, you will not be getting into this party," Thomas is wont to say when a noticeable accumulation of the uninvited have gathered before the ropes. "By knowing you, I mean we have recently had sex and/or brunch this past weekend." This usually makes the point, though there are those who sometimes think they can bribe their way past this stricture.

"Once I was doing the door at the Coral Room and I tried to turn away a couple who were not on the guest list," recalls Thomas. "And the girl said 'Do you think my boyfriend is cute? I'll tell him to make out with you if you let us in.' I politely demurred and suggested they might want to consider couples counseling. Then there are the strangers who will walk up to the ropes and, before even saying a word, begin slipping joints into my back pocket or brazenly offering me bumps of coke, right out in the open. No thanks." Since not all crashers are gifted with celebrity doppelganger properties, some resort to screaming out their star connections—real or imagined— after they've been denied entrance. "One night someone actually yelled at me 'Don't you know who I am? I'm Sandra Bernhard's facialist!' I'm not kidding. And then of course there's the classic standby, 'But I'm Madonna's hairdresser!' Every doorman has heard that one and we all say the same thing: 'Honey, Madonna has *thousands* of hairdressers. *I've* even done her hair!' Soon, there will be crashers showing up saying, 'But I'm Madonna's antiaging physicist!' "

Manhattan is the sort of place where "party crasher" has become its own vocation. There are some who are so good at it, so determined, yet so graceful, that many doormen let them in just because they've become fixtures on the New York party circuit—people who are famous only for crashing parties. "There's that older guy with the poodle hairdo who will go to the opening of a sewer grate," Thomas says. "I always let him in because he's very nice and well behaved and everyone seems to like him."

"Sub-lebrities" are another category of potential party poopers. A term coined by Internet columnist Ed Halter, a sub-lebrity is anyone who has attained a dubious or milieu-specific level of fame. A sub-lebrity could be a club personality, performer, artist, socialite, or beautiful do-nothing. Because there is such a high turnover rate of these small-time stars, Thomas has to be both constantly aware of who they are and on the lookout for the ones with less than golden reputations. "Even if they're known to be kind of messy, I usually have to let them in anyway," Thomas laments. "It's a Courtney Love kind of situation—you're not going to turn her away, and yet you accept the fact that things are probably going to get out of control. I suppose there are things we could do, like tell the bartender to substitute water for vodka in their drinks, or have a cattle prod handy, but for now we usually just rely on our trustworthy security team."

During his door duties, Thomas has to deal with a lot of poorly behaved revelers. Here are the top five offenders.

THE CELEBRITY— "I'll never forget the night that Natasha Lyonne snuck out of Plaid with a bottle of Jack Daniels," remembers Thomas. "The bouncer tried to wrest the bottle from her and a screaming match ensued. I'm sure it was a perfectly honest mistake on her part—when you're trying to unwind and have a good time, it's not always easy to remember what's been paid for and what hasn't."

THE PROMOTER— One night, an event producer was flagrantly snorting coke with members of a former boy band in a bathroom stall. "I was keeping several gossip columnists at bay just outside the bathroom, to avoid the bad press!" Thomas recalls with exasperation. "I stood there bullshitting to them about some upcoming event

Continued

GLENN BELVERIO

One particularly notorious sub-lebrity is the party animal/fashion designer known as Kai Kühne, who is infamous in downtown New York circles for his eccentric attire, his love of booze, and a consistently inappropriate violent temper. A former member of the avant-garde fashion collective, As Four, Kai is not exactly famous outside of the Paris and New York fashion worlds (and perhaps his native Germany). However, because the Paris and New York fashion worlds are viewed by their inhabitants as two Jupiter-sized planets (which are ruled by Karl Lagerfeld and the spirit of Diana Vreeland), in which everything outside of them are but errant asteroid fragments, Kai is able to maintain a certain level of fame. "Of course I'm going to let Kai in," says Thomas. "He's a fixture on the New York party scene and one can't deny that he does indeed 'work a look.'" (Thomas's remark is reminiscent of a 1983 invitation to the legendary New York club, Danceteria, which came in the form of an audio cassette. The club's owner, Rudolf, explains on the cheeky recording: "We are against the Walloons, who are the separatists in Belgium . . . but if the Walloons dress fabulously, we let them in anyway.")

As a result of his surly, drunken behavior,

Kai's outrageous antics have been gleefully doc-
umented by gossip columns such as Page Six of
the *New York Post*. Thomas has been witness to at
least one of these episodes. The club MisShapes
was hosting a party for The Explosion, a neo-
punk quintet from Boston, who were also invited to do a DJ set. "Kai showed up, still on a
seemingly never-ending bender, and told me his
alleged wife-to-be—sub-lebrity Melissa Burns,
formerly of girl group W. I. T.—was meeting
him there later," Thomas recalls. "Some members of The Explosion were in the DJ booth and
had just begun their set as Kai proceeded to get
increasingly drunker. After a few songs, Kai apparently didn't like their taste in music and
stormed over to the DJ booth to share his opin-
ion with members of the band. He did this by
screaming profanities at them and kicking them
in the shins." One of the beautiful things about a
great club story is, because of the confusion created by loud music, dim lighting, crowds, and
booze, many onlookers tend to come away with
slightly different versions of the same event.

"I was standing by the DJ booth while this
was happening," says Leigh Lezark, a member of
the MisShapes. "Kai was dressed in some kind of
white, diaperish outfit . . . I think he was wear-

that they just *had* to attend,
with my body wedged between
them and the bathroom door.
They were standing there,
looking like their bladders
would burst at any moment, it
was like being in a sitcom."

THE DISGRUNTLED REJECT— One
night, a rebuffed Britney
Spears lookalike—who was
turned away simply because
the party was guest list only—
called Thomas "a fucking fairy"
and hurled a chocolate cupcake
at his head. "It was a cupcake
from Magnolia Bakery, so at
least she had some taste,"
Thomas recalls. "The club
bouncer admonished her for
wasting food and sent her
packing."

THE DRUNKEN EJECTS— A group
of rowdy young men were once
thrown out of Coral Room because they were being rude to
the staff. "When I told them to
move away from the door, one
of them broke a beer bottle on
the street and waved it inches
from my face," Thomas recalls
with a shiver. "The bouncer
wrestled him to the ground

Continued

before the ruffian could perform some unorthodox surgery on my nose."

THE TOTAL INEBRIATE— "One night at Squeezebox, a severely inebriated girl, upon exiting the club, walked straight through the ropes without stopping, and dragged the entire shebang out into the middle of the street before collapsing in a pile of metal and velvet," Thomas remembers. "I merely looked down at her and ordered 'Pick it up.'"

ing a toga and a diaper with a G-string underneath. His long hair was dirty and unkempt. He started rubbing up against one of the members of The Explosion—which one I don't know . . . they all look the same to me—and really coming on to him. The guy from the band just kept pushing Kai away and at one point said 'Who is this crazy hippie?!' He didn't know who Kai was, not that it mattered. They got into a shoving match, and then Kai took a swing at him. Geo and Greg went out and got security, who rushed in, grabbed Kai, and threw him out onto the street."

"Security tried to break up the fight and asked Kai to leave," Thomas recalls. "But Kai began to scream and throw punches at the two large bouncers who proceeded to carry him out of the venue on his side as he was flailing his arms and yelling slurred profanities. He was literally tossed out on the sidewalk, his thong underwear hanging out of whatever it was he was wearing, as he continued to swing his arms at the bouncers. The bouncers looked down at him and asked him to leave. Kai got up and stumbled over to a nearby garbage can and made a vain attempt to pick it up and hurl it at the bouncers, but he could barely lift it. And let me tell you, his little show had quite an audience: MTV News correspondent Gideon Yago, Nine Inch Nails bassist Gordi White, Heatherette designer Traver Rains, and supermodel Anouk Lepere. They were all *very* amused. Kai eventually slithered away before bringing any harm to himself or others. A little while later, his voluptuous blonde fiancé, Melissa, arrived and ran around the club and outside on the sidewalk looking for him. After I filled her in on her beau's belligerent behavior, she jumped into a cab to search the city for her man."

Sometimes a sub-lebrity can inadvertently threaten to derail an entire event, as was the case at a Heatherette fashion show where, to further aggravate matters, hordes of crashing bores also showed up en masse . . .

Susanne Bartsch—the legendary party creator and wife of gym chain owner David Barton—is explaining her décor strategy for the upcoming Heatherette fashion show to a flabbergasted production team. "So, I vant to have a man on a trapeze over here, a girl on a rope over there, the jugglers and contortionists on both sides of the runway, the man viz the gorilla suit by the entrance, and the popcorn and cotton candy machines over here, here, and there," Susanne explains in her heavy Swiss-German accent as she points her long, elegant fingers toward various areas of the large space. "Oh, and vee need to ask the building manager if there is room in the elevator so vee can bring in a baby elephant."

Oh my god, Thomas is thinking to himself, *I thought we were just going to extend the runway a few extra feet and slap up some circusy decorations!* Thomas and his assistant Max have been enlisted by MAO PR to production-manage the Heatherette show and help Susanne work out some of the logistics of the circus theme—which has been chosen by Heatherette designers Richie Rich and Traver Rains. Even though Thomas is excited to be working with Susanne for the first time—her reputation as a party hostess comprises a large chunk of New York nightclub history—he begins to feel an aching knot of panic form in his stomach, which then moves swiftly up to his head, stopping at his right temple, where it throbs for the rest of the meeting. *Suppose the elephant charges toward the crowd,* he wonders. *Even the trend spies from knockoff fashion companies who are in the standing section don't deserve to be trampled to death—and how are we going to organize all of this three days before the show?!*

Thomas has worked as both a production manager and doorman for Heatherette in the past, and he knows that even without the threat of flying acrobats and exotic animals, the moments leading up to their shows tend to have an air of chaos and disorganized madness about them. Every season, Richie and Traver can usually be found one week before the show in their studio running around in circles with their hands in the air, shrieking amidst a tornadolike swirl of brightly-colored fabrics, sequins, paint, and glue. On the big day, however, a few minutes before the models step out onto the runway in Heatherette's over-the-top frocks, everything seems to magically come together and the show becomes one of the more memorable events of fashion week. A typical Heatherette show is an enjoyable spectacle that makes the austere runway presentations of Calvin Klein or Ralph Lauren look positively funereal. For this reason, many fashion critics and editors clamor to attend Heatherette's shows, as they are viewed as a welcome break from a hectic work week—a fun recess period after days of serious fashion classes. Unfortunately, editors, celebrities, and other important attendees are not the only ones beating a path to Heatherette's door—the show also attracts probably the largest number of gatecrashers than any other show during fashion week. For this reason, MAO usually employs Thomas and his brand of door bitch crowd control to orchestrate the check-in process. Which means this season Thomas is wearing the hats of production manager, doorman—and possibly elephant wrangler.

"Uh-uh, no way," Max tells Thomas as they are walking down the street after the meeting has finished. "Just pretend you didn't hear her mention the baby elephant, okay? We are *not* bringing live animals into this equation!"

"I've already forgotten about the elephant," Thomas says as he scrolls through the missed calls on his cell phone. "I'm just wondering how the hell we're going to install ropes and trapezes in that space that will be secure enough to hold the weight of the performers!" Thomas calls into his messages and after a few moments of concentrated listening, turns back to Max. "Okay, that was Mauricio at MAO. We need to build a separate dressing room backstage for Boy George," he says with an authoritative tone. "And we need to convert the entire floor above the space where the show will be into a dressing room for Anna Nicole Smith. That means we need to have carpeting put down, couches brought in, and we also need to build a separate multimirrored area for Anna's hair and makeup." Because Richie and Traver idolize Anna Nicole—the designers appeared with her on a special episode of *The Anna Nicole Smith Show*—the zaftig model has been chosen to close this season's show in a special Heatherette look: an outré interpretation of Marilyn Monroe's *Seven Year Itch* dress. What makes this particular runway stint special is that this will be Anna Nicole's first public appearance since she shed at least fifty pounds while on the TrimSpa diet—in fact, the weight loss company will be shuttling their spokesmodel around in a special TrimSpa bus during fashion week. The downsizing pill profiteers will also be filming Anna Nicole sauntering down the catwalk for a TrimSpa commercial.

"Oh, another thing," Thomas tells Max. "We have to be on high alert for parasite paparazzi who might try to sneak into the show . . . they'll be coming out in droves to try to snap Anna Nicole. A photo of her in the *Enquirer* wearing Heatherette might be fine and dandy, but it's more important that we have room for *WWD, Vogue,* and *Bazaar*."

Over the next three days, Thomas, Max, Susanne, and Mauricio busy themselves with the production details of the show. When the big day arrives, the trapezes are hung, the popcorn and cotton candy machines are installed, the space is wrapped in striped circus tent fabric, and the numbered and lettered seats are neatly arranged into rows and sections. Susanne has arranged the cast of acrobats, contortionists, and Pierrotesque clowns into the sort of delirious mise-en-scène that the party queen is famous for. Thomas is stationed at the front of the building with his colleague Theodora, a publicist for Yohji Yamamoto's sport line, Y3, who has signed up to help with the door this evening. Brian, the former PR director of MAO, is making a freelance appearance tonight to also help out. A young intern named Cindy, who is schooled in the who's who of fashion magazine hierarchy, also stands at the ready. Their job is to filter out the uninvited, while checking in legit guests so they can enter the building, proceed to the third floor, and receive their seating assignments.

Thirty minutes before the scheduled show time a huge crowd has gathered. "Oh boy, here we go," Thomas says to Theodora. "The biannual meeting of the Richie Rich Fan Club." A veteran of the New York club kid scene of the early 'nineties, Richie has assembled quite a collection of peers, admirers, and hangers-on—a colorful rogue's gallery of dyed, inked, corseted, and platform-booted creatures of the night. "Some of these kids look like they were cryogenically frozen in 1992 and thawed out this afternoon," a serious-looking woman in a camel's hair coat says to her Chanel-suited friend as the pair make their way toward Thomas. "Hi, we're from Bergdorf Goodman," the woman announces.

"Oh, hi," Thomas says cheerfully, while at the same time warily eyeing the long line of party monsters. "Let me just check you off here . . ." As Thomas is putting a check mark next to each of the buyer's names, his pen suddenly goes skidding across the page, leaving a long, ugly line across the list of guests. "Hi Thomas, love your shirt." A tall man with a towering pink mohawk hairdo, wearing a rhinestone-studded T-shirt and stilettos is shaking Thomas's elbow. "I'm on Richie's list and here are my three guests," the mohawked man says, gesturing toward a trio who are wrapped in layers of voluminous, neon fun fur. They are all of indeterminate gender, age, and livelihood. The woman in the Chanel suit bristles.

"One second guys, these young ladies were here before you, if you don't mind," Thomas says, managing to keep his cool. He shuttles the women into the building and turns to the festive line jumpers. "First of all, there's a line," Thomas says, stating the obvious. "And second of all, this isn't a party, it's a fashion show—no one is allowed to bring guests who did not receive invitations from MAO PR."

"But I'm friends with Richie," the mohawked man protests. "He invited me."

"I understand," Thomas replies. "But there are a lot of people waiting who are friends with Richie. Please get in line and we'll try to accommodate you." The man turns to his furry friends and they stand in a tight circle discussing the situation. They resemble a football huddle at a game between the Muppets and the Park Avenue Ladies.

"My god, why are there so many people here!?" Theodora asks Thomas with astonishment. "There is no way all of these people will fit into that space!"

"Don't worry, a lot of them won't be getting in," Thomas assures her. "This happens every season. Richie and Traver, God bless them, go out every night a week before the show and hand out invitations to all of their friends, as if this were a club event. MAO always tells them not to do that, but do they listen? So all of these kids call the RSVP number—even though they are not on the official invite list—and then e-mail the damn phone number to their network of friends who in turn all call in and RSVP. It's a nightmare!" As Thomas is explaining this to her, a man with long black hair styled in ringlets strides confidently past the long line and straight up to the check-in team. He's wearing black vinyl pants and a black sequined shirt which is unbuttoned to his navel; a tattoo of Betty Boop reinvented as a leather-clad dominatrix, which adorns the pale, lean flesh of his left pectoral muscle, peaks out from behind the shirt.

"Are you on the list?" Thomas asks him as he turns up the power on his gate-crasher force field. "I'm friends with Richie, I have a seat in the front row," the man tells him with an affected, queenly lilt. When he notices a look of hostile skepticism sweep across Thomas's face, he taps his well-manicured, fuchsia-painted index fingernail on the metal clamp of the clipboard. "No, really—check the list." Thomas gets his name, flips through a few pages of the list, and, lo and behold, the man is telling the truth. "I'm really sorry," Thomas says, apologizing for his face muscles. "Go right in."

Over the next twenty minutes the frenzy heightens, as the flamboyantly dressed, mascara-ed masses make various appeals to Thomas, Theodora, and Brian. "But I'm friends with Richie!" is their battle cry, much as "but I'm friends with Paris Hilton!" is the number-one slogan shouted outside some of the clubs Thomas works at. "Thomas, darling!" An androgynous life form that looks like the love child of Barbarella and Hello Kitty zeros in on Thomas for an air kiss. "Spare me, sweetheart," Thomas growls at this person he has never met before. "Get in line!"

"Oh my goodness!" Theodora gasps with exasperation as she wards off the colorful army of show crashers. "This is a fashion show, *not* Motherfucker!" The twenty-first-century club kids are not the only fashion imposters, either. "I'm Merle Ginsberg," a tall, beautiful black woman says assertively, referring to the former entertainment editor of *W* Magazine.

"But Merle Ginsberg is a petite Jewish lady," Thomas corrects her. Photographers are also a part of the Heatherette mania, as dozens of shutterbugs show up with Anna Nicole dollar signs gleaming in their eyes. "I'm from *TV Guide*," one camera-schlepping schlub tells Thomas.

"Thank you very much," Thomas says curtly while imperiously pointing the way for the photographer—away from the entrance and back toward the street. Other photographers who are also given the bum's rush by Thomas begin making furious cell phone calls to their would-be bosses. "Bonnie Fuller, please," one photog shouts over the din into his phone. "Tell her it's the guy who got those shots of Kirstie Alley coming out of the Weight Watchers meeting last week." Meanwhile, Cindy the intern is busy squeezing between the groups of lacquered and painted personalities who have wandered away from the line and congregated in front of Thomas. Her mission: Find the editors and buyers and hustle them through the door and into the elevator. "I've got Brooke from *WWD!*" Cindy hollers to Thomas and Theodora as she pushes through a cluster of startled goth girls with Brooke close behind.

With five minutes till the alleged show time—fashion shows never start on schedule—Thomas makes an announcement. "If there is anyone waiting in line who knows they have a seat assignment, please come see us now!" A Japanese woman, who turns out to be a buyer from Barneys Tokyo, leaves the line and scurries quickly up to Theodora and Brian. The clans of club kids, most of whom have already faced the Door Bitch's ire, stay put—even if they still seem determined to get into the show. After Cindy escorts a few more late-arriving fashion critics through the door, Thomas receives a call on his headset from Mauricio. "Thomas, we have to start the show soon. We're full to capacity—close the doors and come upstairs with the rest of the door crew so you can help us with the final seating." Without looking back at the long line of shut-outs, Thomas and the team close the doors behind them and pile into the elevator.

When the doors open on the third floor and reveal the pandemonium that's in full swing, it makes the scene outside look like a senior citizen bingo night. In the lobby, a mob of people are pressed up against madly percolating popcorn and wildly spinning cotton candy machines as they wait for their seating assignments in front of the check-in table. Behind the table an entire wall of video monitors is flashing a rapidly changing series of messages: "MAO Space," "Heatherette," "New York Fashion Week," while in front of the monitors a girl in a gold Lurex bikini is swinging widely back and forth on a rope.

"Ladies and gentlemen, welcome to Heatherette!" Max is broadcasting through a microphone. "Please move into your seats or the standing section so we can start the show!" One of the jugglers, who is riding atop the shoulders of a fellow juggler, drops one of his rubber balls and it bounces off Max's head, hitting the fashion critic from *The Daily Telegraph*. "Blimey!" she exclaims. "It's like a war zone in here!" Thomas pushes his way through the crowd and makes his way over to Max, who is standing between the end of the runway and the photographer's pit. Max starts walking toward Thomas but is suddenly distracted by a disruption amongst the photographers. "I need to be right here so I can get my shots!" A man with thinning hair and a large nose is screaming at the other photographers as he struggles to push them aside and make room for himself at the front of the group. A shoving match ensues and Max and Thomas rush over to the pit. Thomas immediately recognizes the man with the large nose as notorious paparazzo, Steve Sands.

"Oh god, how did *he* get in here?!" Thomas asks Max. "He must have spent the night here, because I *know* I didn't see him outside during the check-in." Sands is infamous for his troublesome behavior at celebrity events, and has resorted to such stunts as yelling out Demi Moore's home address to fellow paparazzi when the actress refused to pose for him on a red carpet.

"Listen, you can't do that," Max tells Sands. "A lot of these guys have assigned spots and they're shooting for major fashion publications."

"What are you going to do, call security?" Sands challenges.

"That's exactly what I'm going to do," Max says. He immediately summons two security guards and explains the situation to them. They grab Sands, drag him out of the pit, and begin hauling him toward the exit. "You can't do this to me!" he screams. "I'm going to call the police!" A man in a gorilla suit, who has been faux boxing with a clown near the runway, begins jumping up and down and making gleeful monkey noises as the pesky paparazzo is dragged away. Max shouts through his microphone at the ersatz chimp. "Calm down, Mighty Joe Young," he reprimands him.

"It looks like you have everything under control," Thomas says to Max.

"I'm doing my best," Max says as he moves aside to allow

New York's most photographed dandy, Patrick McDonald, squeeze by to get to his seat. McDonald is wearing a striped, burnt orange, double-breasted suit and a scarlet fedora. Trailing behind him are Mickey Boardman and Kim Hastreiter from *Paper* Magazine. "But you better go talk to Aimee—she told me a few minutes ago that Drew hasn't shown up yet, and she was freaking out," Max tells Thomas.

"Oh god, let me go find her," Thomas says. Aimee Phillips is Heatherette's studio manager and a member of the club promoter trio The Trinity. The very essence of sub-lebrity, Aimee and her partners Macky Dugan and Drew Elliott are self-appointed tastemakers of New York nightlife. Together, they are determined to bring back old-school nightlife glamour to what they perceive to be the lackluster state of the club world. They do this by throwing parties at various clubs where other ambitious sub-lebrities—who eschew the self-destructive habits of their club kid predecessors—mingle, self-promote, and enter each other's contact info into their Sidekicks.

Because of their important sub-lebrity status, it is a tradition that the Trinity always be seated together in the front row of every Heatherette show—in fact, it would be considered an omen of bad luck if this detail of the seating chart were to change. "Thomas, we have a major problem," Aimee says in a panicked voice, when Thomas finally locates her behind a gaggle of contortionists. "Drew just called me—he's stuck downstairs! We really need you to go down there and get him in."

"But Aimee, the door is closed," Thomas tells her. "And the

show is going to start in two minutes!" While he's speaking, his cell phone rings. It's Drew. "Thomas, I'm stuck downstairs, please come get me!" *Oh god, this is all I need!* Thomas thinks. "Okay, Drew—I'm on my way down." As production manager of the show, Thomas knows that the backstage crew, the lighting team, and the models really can't make a move until he, Mauricio, and Brian collectively give the green light. As Thomas is riding down the elevator, Max's voice crackles to life in his headset. "Thomas, where the hell did you go? We need to start the show *now!*"

"No Max, you need to hold the show—I have to get Drew in!" The elevator doors open and Thomas rushes through the glass doors of the building and out to the sidewalk, where he is only half surprised to see the entire line of gate-crashers still wrapped around the block. "Drew, where the hell are you? Get your ass over here!" Thomas spots the willowy, black suit–clad sub-lebrity, grabs him by the arm and yanks him through the entrance and into the elevator. As the doors close Thomas, who is now breathing heavily, looks at him and says, "You really owe me brunch for this."

"Brunch? What are you, some kind of gay superhero?" Drew replies.

"Listen to me, Drew—when we get inside we need to *run* to your seat as quickly as possible, do you understand? The show was supposed to start ten minutes ago." The elevator doors open and Thomas pushes Drew out, grabs his arm, and pulls him through the check-in lobby and toward the front row. As

they are entering the main area—*pow!*—one of the swinging
trapeze artists accidentally kicks Thomas in the head as he
moves toward the empty seat with the tardy sub-lebrity in tow.
The house has darkened and the runway is awash in bright
spotlights by the time they reach the seat. Thomas whips Drew
around and flings him in place, jamming him between Aimee
and Macky. The second Thomas dashes away from the runway
and into the darkness, the show begins.

The show's MC, Boy George, emerges dressed in a boxy
jacket embellished with colored string, trousers covered with
prints and patches, and an outsized hat with a jutting brim. As
he glides down the runway, the pop icon resembles a battleship
that has cruised through a crowded King's Road clothing shop
and, undeterred, has continued down the trendy boulevard,
unaware of the flotsam and jetsam its hull has accumulated
along the way. As he introduces the show, his voice still sounds
as golden and dewy as it did when he first crooned "Do You
Really Want to Hurt Me?" to hordes of swooning teeny-
boppers and lonely housewives. He takes a seat by the runway
and provides running commentary as the models begin marching out. Heatherette's fashion message this season appears to be
the result of corralling groups of clowns, cowgirls, Hollywood
rent boys, and Pigalle streetwalkers into an enormous fun
house barrel. After adding heaps of metallic fabric, unnaturally
colored wigs, Pop Art canvases, and the wardrobe from the film
Showgirls into the barrel, the captives and contents are spun at
high speed for one hour and then spilled out onto the runway.

The result is a wacky, sublime pageant that looks like a Venetian ball art directed by Timothy Leary.

"This is *so* genius," Thomas enthuses to Theodora as they stand toward the back taking in the show. "Those kids really know how to pull it all together." After iconic male model Markus Schenkenberg is trotted out shirtless, Heatherette's pneumatic transsexual muse—Amanda Lepore—makes an appearance in a red trapeze artist's leotard. Bringing up the rear of this extravaganza is the slimmed-down Anna Nicole, who caps the show by mouthing some of the words to "Diamonds are a Girl's Best Friend," which is playing on the show's sound track. Whistles and applause erupt from the audience. "This is boring. Where's the baby elephant I ordered?" Max jokes to Thomas after he finds him standing in the back.

"You're right," says Thomas, "the crowd's disappointment over the lack of elephants is palpable. We've failed as production managers." After Richie and Traver take their bow, the guests—behaving as if they're on an ether high—abandon their seats to indulge in cotton candy and to rub up against some the shirtless male acrobats who are roaming the space. "I could eat about ten cotton candies right now," Thomas tells Max before he heads backstage to continue his role as production manager.

Not all party disruptions come from sub-lebrities. Sometimes, ordinary party people can earn their fifteen minutes of infamy when alcohol and an overzealous attitude toward rock stars are combined . . .

The curvy Latino girl in low-rider jeans and a tight T-shirt is pleading her case to Geo outside MisShapes, where Jarvis Cocker of the band Pulp is the evening's headlining DJ. "Please, please, please, you have to let me in to see Jarvis! I flew all the way here from San Francisco for just one night so I could see him!" Geo stands mannequinlike in front of her, dressed in a black Helmut Lang T-shirt and matching nylon Martin Margiela vest. Because his long bangs cover his eyes entirely, it's impossible to tell if he's indifferent or sympathetic to the girl's plight. After all, the club is packed and Thomas has already ordered an iron-fisted proclamation: Regulars and VIPs only. "The doorman won't let me and my friend in. Do you think you can talk to him?" she says. Geo remains motionless for a few more moments, as if lost in thought, and then begins to move toward Thomas like a wax figure that has magically come to life within a hipster diorama. "Thomas, this girl flew all the way here from San Francisco to see Jarvis—you should let her in."

"Bullshit!" Thomas huffs when Geo delivers the news. The girl walks over to Thomas. "It's true, I flew here because I heard he was in America and I never got to see Pulp," the girl says, excitement and hope rising in her voice. "I'm a huge Jarvis Cocker and Pulp fan—I just want to see him!"

"Please, you did not fly here from San Francisco," Thomas says, not budging on his position. "You're full of shit." Without saying another word, the girl reaches into her purse and pulls out a plane ticket and presents it to Thomas. "SF to NYC 2/5/05, NYC to SF 2/6/05" it reads. Thomas's stubborn heart seems to grow in size, like a reformed grinch. "You know, you're really cute. I think that's so amazing—you're a totally dedicated fan! Go on in, I hope you and your friend have a great time," Thomas says and waives the cover fee for them.

Inside the club on the second floor, Jarvis and fellow band member Steve Mackey have just taken the DJ booth and are spinning "Turn It Out" from the band Death From Above 1979. Jarvis's wife, Camille, is standing in the DJ booth with them, surveying the crowd of appreciative dancers. Right before the Pulp boys began their set, the San Francisco girl and her friend busied themselves at the bar by downing shots and congratulating themselves for getting past the doorman. The moment Jarvis begins commandeering the decks, the self-proclaimed number-one fan rushes over to the booth and stands directly in front of it, leaving her friend behind to gyrate on the crowded dance floor. She stands there enraptured, studying every one of Jarvis's moves, from the way he pushes his

INSIDE/OUTSIDE—TWO VIEWS OF A NIGHTLIFE STORY

One of the great things about a good, gossipy nightclub anecdote is that it often takes several eyewitnesses to piece together the chain of events. Here, Thomas tells the story of the night My Chemical Romance DJed at MisShapes, with the help of his pal Sarah Lewitinn, aka Ultragrrrl—the twenty-five-year-old blogger, DJ, music journalist, and founder of the record label Stolen Transmission.

SHE SAID:
"I was hanging out with my friend Andrew by the DJ booth while Mikey and Gerard were DJing . . . Mikey was my first boyfriend when I was eighteen, and then a few years later I was My Chem's manager for awhile. So, the rest of the band was standing near the booth with us when we noticed this girl who was very androgynous—dressed all in black, combat boots, with lots of black makeup but very short hair—lingering around the band. She reminded me of someone you would see in a

Continued

heavy-framed glasses back up his nose to his long fingers twisting the knobs on the soundboard. Halfway through "Club Foot" by Kasabian, Camille motions for Geo to come over to the DJ booth.

"Geo, that girl is really making me nervous—she keeps staring at Jarvis and she won't leave that spot!" she tells him. "She's very ominous."

"Okay, I'll tell her to stop standing there," Geo reassures her and when he turns to find the girl, he notices she's moved up and placed her arm around the wooden edge of the booth. "I'm sorry, you have to get back a little bit," he tells her. "You can't stand this close to the booth." The girl ignores him and hugs the wooden edge of the booth tighter. When Geo opens the door and enters the DJ booth, the girl aggressively puts her foot in, preventing him from closing it. "You have to remove yourself from here right now!" Geo shouts at her.

Camille begins to panic. "I'm getting out of here!" she shrieks and makes a move to leave the booth. Like a small dog trying to dart through an open screen door, the girl attempts to run between Camille's legs and into the booth. "Oh my god, she's crazy! Stop her!" Camille yells. Geo

quintessential goth video. She kept getting closer and closer to the band in this really creepy way, but she wouldn't say anything, and I was thinking *If you're going to get that close, at least try to be friendly—make an attempt at a conversation.* She was kind of freaking me out so I grabbed Andrew and we started dancing between her and the band, to try to drive her away, but that didn't work, because she kept maneuvering around us to get closer to them.

"Finally, Brian—My Chem's manager—went over to her and said 'You have to go away,' and that scared her off for a bit. Then a little while later, I went over to the bar to get a drink and she was sitting there sobbing into a glass of red wine! Her tears and black eye makeup were literally dripping down her face and into the glass. I felt bad for her! It was so *very* My Chemical Romance! So, I got a drink and go into the DJ booth to hang out with Mikey and Gerard, and the girl comes back and stands directly in front of the booth . . . she's

Continued

thinks fast and grabs the girl around the waist and drags her out of the booth. "Camille, close the door! I'm going to get security!" Camille slams the booth door shut and puts her body against it. She resembles a potential victim in a slasher flick trying to keep a psycho killer at bay. Geo runs outside and a few minutes later returns with a large security guard. At this point the girl is in the middle of climbing over the top of the booth and Camille has placed her body between her and Jarvis.

Unfazed, Jarvis continues spinning, looking down at the soundboard with a frozen gaze. He puts on "Ladyfingers" by The Fever and the crowd continues dancing. The guard reaches into the booth and drags the girl out by her legs and waist. She begins flailing her arms around and screaming at the top of her lungs. "Let go of me, you asshole!" As Geo is helping the guard lift her out of the booth, she hits Geo in the face and grabs his Helmut Lang shirt by the neck and starts pulling. Geo smacks her on the back of the head and she lets go, but she continues screaming and swinging as the guard hauls her across the dance floor and down the stairs.

Back outside, Thomas is chatting with a friend when the doors to the club burst open and

holding on to the glass shield that protects the soundboard, staring at them and crying. She was gawking at them like they were circus animals! She looked like she could have been nearly thirty—a little too long in the tooth to be behaving this way. I told her to stop holding on to the glass and she let go and started crying even more.

"Brian had just had it at this point. He told her, 'You need to leave or we're going to throw you out.' But she wouldn't move, so Brian got one of the bouncers who helped him try to get the girl out. They started taking her down the stairs that are near the DJ booth and she grabbed onto one of the speakers that are mounted on the wall. She was literally hanging there, and before the bouncer could pull her off, she let go and dropped to the floor and laid there motionless... she became like a body. Word spread through the club that the bouncers were scuffling with some 'goth dude.' Then the bouncer and Brian tried to lift

Continued

Geo, the bouncer and the girl come exploding out. "You fucking asshole! Put me down!" Still in the grip of the bouncer, the girl swats her free arm in the direction of the hand stamp station and sends several rubber stamps and ink pads sailing onto the sidewalk. "I need to go back in and see Jarvis! Put me the fuck down!"

Thomas's jaw drops. "Oh . . . my . . . god." The guard dumps her on the sidewalk and she begins sobbing uncontrollably. "You can't do that, it's completely inappropriate," Geo reprimands her. "You can't go into a DJ booth like that."

After a few moments, Geo and the bouncer leave the girl and walk over to Thomas and explain to him what happened. "Great," Thomas says. "I let her in out of the graciousness of my own heart and she goes from being this nice, devoted fan to a screaming psycho stalker, all in the space of less than one hour!"

"Must have been that demon alcohol," the bouncer jokes. "I haven't seen a fan react that way since that time I saw a gay guy cry when he met Celine Dion at a red carpet event I was working at!"

"Jesus, I feel really duped," Thomas says before Geo goes back inside to check on Camille

her and suddenly she gets up and bolts out of the club."

HE SAID:

"I saw her leave and the bouncer told me what happened and then about an hour later, she came back. She seemed pretty wasted and she told me she needed to get back in the club so she could get a cigarette and I was, like, 'huh?' So I told her, 'I can't let you back in, you were asked to leave,' and she looked at me like she's going to burst into tears. Then she walked away from me over to the side of the club and I looked over and suddenly she fell into one of the potted shrubs that are near the wall! She was struggling to get up, holding on to the branches of the shrub, nearly uprooting the entire plant—and then she gets on her feet and *wham!* She falls over onto the sidewalk, right where people wait in line to get into the club. People were stepping over and around her and a few said 'Oh, there's that goth dude who was such a mess inside!'

"The bouncer went over to

Continued

and Jarvis. About fifteen minutes later, the girl returns to the door. She is still sobbing hysterically. "I really want to come back inside," she pleads, with more than a slight drunken slur in her voice.

"I'm really sorry, but I can't let you back in," says Thomas. The girl starts crying harder. "I need to fucking get back in there, don't be an asshole, please let me back inside!" she pleads.

"Listen, they told me what happened inside," Thomas says sternly. "Jarvis is really uncomfortable. You're done for the night. You really cannot come back in, I'm sorry."

"You're a fucking asshole, man! You're a really *bad* person . . . you ruined my trip . . . you ruined my life!" she screams. The bouncer who has just thrown her out overhears her rant and starts making a move toward her. She backs off, walks a few yards away from the door, and collapses on the curb with her head between her knees and returns to her incessant sobbing.

Two hours go by. The girl is still doubled over on the curb crying hysterically when Geo comes out to talk to Thomas. "Jarvis and Camille want to leave now but they're concerned that that girl might still be here," Geo tells him. Thomas silently points in the direction of the

her to see if she was okay and said 'We can't revive her, she's out cold' and I didn't believe it. It seemed like a desperate ploy for attention—a performance so she could get back in the club. So I was standing there rolling my eyes, saying loudly 'Will someone *please* tell the passed out girl that My Chemical Romance has *left* the building and they are no longer here!' And the bouncer was throwing cold water on her face and she still wasn't coming to, and he was, like, 'I think we need to call an ambulance,' and I then I felt bad for behaving like such an asshole. So the ambulance arrives about fifteen minutes later and the paramedics were finally able to revive her with some smelling salts . . . and when she woke up, she burst into tears and pleaded 'please help me, please help me.' It was very dramatic. Then the paramedics put her head in a brace, strapped her to a board, and took her away in the ambulance."

sobbing stalker. "Holy crap, she's *still* here!" Geo says, flabbergasted.

"Oh yeah," Thomas replies "She's been a one-woman Wailing Wall for the past two hours. Let me go to the corner and hail a cab for Jarvis and then you can shuttle him and Camille out and into safety . . . maybe if they tiptoe quickly and quietly, she won't notice them." Thomas flags down a cab and, sure enough, Jarvis and his wife escape into it unscathed. "Another night, another rabid fan," Thomas says to the bouncer. "Maybe the club should consider installing an electric fence around that DJ booth." He looks over at the sobbing girl and notices she's pulled her plane ticket out of her purse and is holding it close to her face, as if trying to make out the details. Suddenly, she leaps up and bolts into the street with her arm in the air. She does this so quickly, she nearly gets hit by a car. "Oh god," Thomas says to the bouncer. "I think she's just realized she's late for her flight back to San Francisco." Thomas runs over to her, guides her back to the sidewalk and—proving again that the Door Bitch does indeed have a heart—hails a cab for her and pours her into the backseat.

Thomas at the door of Squeezebox with *Cheri Currie* of *The Runaways*. "I was so thrilled to meet one of rock 'n' roll's first female stars."

Front row rock stars: *Debbie Harry* and *Miss Guy* front and center at Boy George's B-Rude fashion show. Thomas (left) produced the show.

The door scene outside of
MOTHERFUCKER.
PHOTO BY MARO

Thomas with MOTHERFUCKER
founder *Michael T.* "Michael's Rocky
Horror homage is legendary."
LASTNIGHTSPARTY.COM

Chi Chi Valenti holds sway over
the crowd at MOTHERFUCKER's
5th Anniversary party.
PHOTO BY MARO

Hilary Duff DJing at MisShapes.
"I was impressed with Hilary's set."

Jarvis Cocker of the band *Pulp* (right) with wife
Camille Bidault-Waddington at MisShapes.
"Jarvis was harassed by an obsessed
fan the night he DJed at the club."

Brandon Flowers, lead singer of *The Killers*,
with Sarah Lewitinn, a.k.a. Ultragrrrl

Madonna made a surprise DJ appearance at MisShapes. "Her remix of 'Everybody' was amazing. Meeting 'M' was one of the highlights of my career."

Thomas was at the door the night of **Courtney Love's** infamous performance at Plaid. "Despite her messiness, Courtney is a much-needed female presence in the rock world. Her unpredictable nature makes for a great show."
LIBERATION LANNILLO, TRIGGER-MAGAZINE

Diddy and *Felix da Housecat* whipped the crowd into a frenzy at the Winter Music Conference in Miami. "It was a surprise meeting of haute hip-hop royalty and under-the-radar electro-house."

MOTHERFUCKER party producers Johnny T., Justine D., Michael T., and Georgie Seville

MisShapes promoters and DJs Greg.K, Geordon Nicol (a.k.a. Geo), and Leigh Lezark

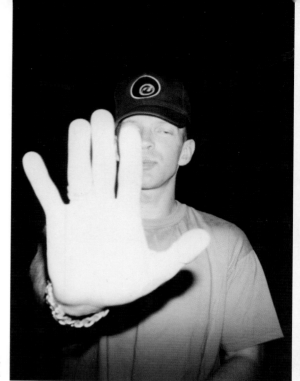

Derek Neen, gatekeeper to the Roxy, banishes undesirables from the the door.

Door diva **Kenny Kenny** guards the entrance to the long-defunct Disco 2000 at The Limelight. "Kenny Kenny is ground zero for a lot of the things I do in my job."

"Spikey" Phil Meynell with Thomas at
Club Revolver in Miami. "I looked like
Phil's Puerto Rican wife."
PHOTO BY EDDIE NEWTON FOR NEWYORKNIGHTS.COM

Thomas finally gets some sleep, along with
MisShapes' Greg.K, during the ride back to his
Miami hotel. "Please note my prodigious man-boob."
PHOTO BY SEAN DACK

Thomas in his Dario Argento T-shirt, a gift from the author.
LASTNIGHTSPARTY.COM

7 .

Fame, it's not your brain, it's just the flame
That burns your change to keep you insane.
—DAVID BOWIE

f Madonna deejays at MisShapes, then *Jesus Christ* will DJ here next week!" Lauren, who is one half of the twenty-one-year-old party girl sisters, The Twins, pants hyperbolically. With her bleached blonde hair and retro attire, Lauren channels Ms. Ciccone's mideighties' look. "This is better than Studio 54!" she adds with a curious lack of irony. Pop stars have been on par with or bigger than Mr. Christ since the Beatles—acutely aware of the irony—pointed out this fact and cemented rock 'n' pop as the next religion.

The DJ gig *du moment*—a ploy for Madonna to promote *Confessions on a Dance Floor* to younger music consumers via the club's cool cred ripple effect—is further proof that recording artists are like celestial bodies: the force of their gravitational pull is in direct correlation to the size of their mass, or rather, their mass appeal. Since Thomas is New York's top doorman, he often finds himself directly in the path of that gravitational pull. "The only reason you're getting in is because you are *you* and you should remember that," Thomas says sternly to an acquaintance who is trying to negotiate the entrance of three friends. "Your friends are not you. And I'm not letting them in."

Due to the small size of the venue and the (metaphorically) large size of the celestial body—who has just been whisked through the side entrance with her producer Stuart Price and several body guards—the crowd of young hipsters, older Madonna fans, and tourists, requires weeding out with repeated, forceful blows of a razor-sharp scythe. "If you are not a regular or not on the VIP list, you will *not* be getting in tonight!" Thomas, donned in a Unabomber-style hood, announces ad nauseum to the mob of people shivering under hundreds of umbrellas in the pouring rain.

When the woman who has ruled over pop music's kingdom for a period of time that seems to rival a despot's unchallenged term enters the DJ booth, the club's second floor is packed so tightly that it is feared it may collapse. "Everyone needs to just *calm* down and stop pushing," Madonna implores the crowd that has surged toward her, threatening to crush both diva and DJ booth.

"I'm really glad to be here and you're going to hear some great music, but can you move back a bit first? A girl's gotta breathe!" The volume of the pop queens's modified Farrah Fawcett/curling-ironed hairdo—a style that once teetered precariously between the Death of Disco and the Birth of New Wave—lends a bobblehead doll look to the diminutive diva.

Stuart Price begins playing a set of songs from Madonna's new album and past oeuvre and the singer smiles broadly, teeth and lip gloss gleaming in the camera lights. When a tweaked version of "Everybody" comes on, Madge begins moving to the beat and waving her arms, recalling the scene in *Desperately Seeking Susan* when the then-embryonic star danced to "Into the Groove" on the floor of Danceteria. Younger members of the crowd gawk as if she's the Eighth Wonder of the World, while the older fans dance ecstatically. A few burst into tears. One hour later, the holy rites have finished and the queenly quadragenarian is outside at the ropes. *"That was amazing!"* she tells Thomas. "It meant the world to me to see everyone so into it!" And then the former, current, and future Material Girl was off.

Needless to say, Thomas's door duties have intersected with the glitzy, giddy world of recording stars more times than he can even remember—a dizzying panoply of hip-hop tycoons, punk princesses, digital demimondaines, and successful close friends. From his early, starstruck encounter with Debbie Harry in the coat check room at Squeezebox ("My Blondie T-shirt caught her eye"), to the night Marilyn Manson made an appearance at the same club in 1996 ("Six months after he was at Squeezebox, he appeared in his music videos and on his record covers looking like an amalgamation of all the freaks he was studying at the club"), to more recent dalliances during his door-god duties, Thomas has crossed paths with many an icon. As guardian of the gates through which these stars pass, he is sometimes called upon to leave that self-proclaimed capital of the media world—Manhattan—such as the time recording artists, DJs, and professional drinkers descended upon the Sunshine State . . .

"So you guys are called the MisShapes, huh?" the Adidas rep says to the motley crew gathered before her. "You look more like the *Rough* Shapes!"

Thomas and fellow doorman Phil, along with Geo, Greg.K and Leigh—the DJs and party-throwers known as the MisShapes—are at the Shore Hotel in Miami Beach, squinting in the sun-drenched room that Adidas is using as a temporary showroom. Hungover and bleary-eyed from last night's work and revelry—a block party hosted by Bacardi rum—this downtown New York quintet is decidedly not ready for its closeup. Being that Adidas is sponsoring a party at the 2005 Winter Music Conference, where Thomas and Phil will work the door and the MisShapes will spin, the hard-partying New Yorkers have all been requested to come attired in Adidas. The rep disappears into the bedroom for a few moments and returns bearing a shopping bag with "Thomas Onorato" magic-markered onto an attached white sticker. "It's really 'gay,' just like you requested," she says with uncertainty as she holds the bag up in front of Thomas. "Let me know if it's okay. I can always get you something different."

She opens the bag and pulls out a white nylon jacket that is adorned with gray rectangles accented with turquoise and pink triangles, and she holds it up for Thomas's approval. The garish track jacket is a dead ringer for the one worn by Bea Arthur on *The Golden Girls* circa 1987. "Oh my god, it's *so* genius!" Thomas enthuses, basking in the garment's unadulterated camp value.

"I'm glad you like it," the girl says, eyeballing Thomas with a look of both skepticism and cautious admiration. "And I have the outfits for the rest of you guys, too—hold on." She runs back into the bedroom and returns with a pink tracksuit with metallic gold stripes for Phil, and an assortment of boy-sized shorts, tank tops, jackets, and bathing suits. The Mis-Shapes dive in like Miami Beach matrons at a yard sale.

The gang has been invited to work and party at the 2005 Miami Winter Music Conference by Tommy Saleh, the creative director of the Tribeca Grand—a New York hotel known for its hip DJ and live performance events. The music at Saleh's events during this period falls into an amorphous genre—electro-retro-disco with a dash of laptop pop that seems to have sprung from the synthesized loins of seminal 'seventies and 'eighties bands like Kraftwerk, Suicide, and Cabaret Voltaire. The Tribeca Grand/Adidas party—which will take place in a dodgy area of Miami, far from the idyll of South Beach, at a club called the Pawn Shop—will mostly showcase DJs who spin hard and serious techno-electro, with a few live bands such as Radio 4 and Cut Copy rounding out the bill.

The New York crew arrives at the Pawn Shop at around nine-thirty P.M., and Thomas and Phil take their positions at the door and begin looking over the guest list. Because they have been in Miami for nearly a week, Thomas's New York

FIVE TIPS ON DOING THE DOOR FOR A ROCK STAR PARTY

"Having Thomas at the door gives your party a stamp of approval," Carlos D., the bassist for the band Interpol, once told *Spin* Magazine on the occasion of his thirtieth birthday celebration. "I wanted it done by a professional."

Here are five ways to master the gig with door bitch panache.

1. WEAR SOMETHING THAT EXUDES AUTHORITY. "I chose a black Marc Jacobs military jacket, complete with epaulettes, so the unruly crowd would know who was in charge."

2. COMPLIMENT THE BIRTHDAY BOY'S OR GIRL'S OUTFIT CHOICE. "On that night, Carlos was wearing a black mod suit, a red shirt, and a black tie. We call it the 'Kraftwerk Carlos' look."

Continued

nightlife pallor has evolved into a Donatella Versace–like tan. He's made the mistake of applying light concealer under his eyes that no longer matches his skin tone—a mistake commonly made by many amateur Latino drag queens. This effect, combined with his shiny, shellacked bangs that sweep down over one side of his face, causes his pink-and-gold-garbed companion to declare: "Thomas, you look like my Puerto Rican wife!" After several minutes of sidesplitting laughter, the door of the club opens and Tommy Saleh pops his head out. "Guys, just so you know, Diddy might come," Saleh says of the artist formerly known as Puff Daddy. Because the Adidas party is a white dance music as opposed to black hip-hop event, Thomas and Phil are completely unconvinced that his Diddyness would bother gracing this party with his presence.

"Yeah, right," Thomas says after Saleh leaves. He pulls out a compact mirror and makes a futile attempt to blend his concealer in. "I'll believe it when I see it." Behind the closed door, they can hear Saleh having a loud argument with the club's manager. Soon, guests—music industry people dressed in khaki shorts, New York and Miami hipsters, and VIPs—begin lining up in front of Thomas and Phil, while the club's in-house doorman lets in a few members of the non-VIP public who pay to enter. Shortly after Thomas and Phil begin checking in people who are on the list, the manager of the club comes out. "You can't let anyone else in right now, tell everyone they're going to need to wait," he says gruffly.

"What? But there are important music editors out here!" Thomas gestures toward Josh Glazer, the editor of *URB,* and Rob Simas, the editor of *BPM,* who are at the front of the line. "I can't make these people wait! These are the kind of guests who are *never* made to wait!"

"Too bad. They're gonna have to wait. I'll let you know when you can let a few more people in. You get me?" With that he turns and walks back into the club.

"I'm so sorry," Thomas says with exasperation to the annoyed pair, who happen to be the two biggest dance music editors in the country. "We'll try to get you in as soon as possible." Over the next few hours the door scene turns into a virtual hostage situation: every ten or fifteen minutes the club's manager inexplicably allows Thomas and Phil to let in only *one* guest, but only after minutes of negotiation. "But this

3. SHOW UP ON TIME. "Actually, I was thirty minutes late and the security guards had to part the Red Sea in the crowded downstairs waiting area to install me at my door post!"

4. KNOW WHICH OTHER ROCK STARS ARE COMING AND WHAT THEY LOOK LIKE. "Carlos actually asked me 'So, you know what the rest of my band looks like, right? And you know what The Strokes look like?' Puhleaze!"

5. ATTEND THE PARTY AFTER YOUR DOOR SHIFT IS OVER. "I always love seeing the select crowd having a good time after all that chaos and aggravation at the door. This party was very private and the balance of music and energy was perfect. Even I got drunk!"

is James Murphy's wife!" Thomas pleads, tears of frustration cutting a trail through his too-white concealer. "James is one of the headlining DJs!" Every few minutes, Saleh comes out and loudly argues with the manager, to no avail.

Finally, at two A.M., after hours of begging, arguing, crying—not to mention sweating beneath their nylon tracksuits—Thomas and Phil are able to get the VIP guests— the ones who haven't stormed away in disgust—into the club. "That was very fucked up," Thomas says, exhausted. "I've never been so mortified in front of so many important people." Just then, one of the night's greatly anticipated DJs, Felix da Housecat, shows up at the entrance of the club. As Thomas is lifting the rope, Felix announces to him and Phil, "Listen, Diddy is right behind me." The two track-suited doormen give each other dubious glances. "He must've been kidding," Thomas says.

Five minutes later, however, Thomas turns around and brushes his bangs away from his left eye so he can be certain he's seeing what he thinks he's seeing. Standing politely at the front of the VIP line, dressed in white pants, a white button-down shirt, white sneakers, and white baseball cap—and not saying a word—is Diddy. Behind him is his flashy, yet equally polite, entourage. There are no limos pulled up to the front of the club, no fanfare, no elbowing paparazzi, no trumpet-blowing, bling-bling-laden angels descending on a gold lamé cloud from Heaven to herald Diddy's holy hip-hop presence. In other words, it was a subtle arrival. "Hey, I'm Diddy," he says to a flummoxed Thomas, who shakes his hand.

He then proceeds to introduce his entourage, but the names are all a blur to Thomas: some guy named Danger, DJ so-and-so, "my girl," this girl, that girl, that record executive. All of them are dressed to the nines, with the girls playing that careful balancing act between classy and slutty. The last person in the entourage is a name most certainly recognizable to Thomas—the famed hip-hop producer, Timbaland, who has worked with Missy Elliott, Alicia Keys, Brandy, Jay Z, and scores of others, and who commands a fee of up to $275,000 per track.

Diddy and his entourage are whisked into the club, where the manager and his minions are already bolting toward the VIP room to clear the way. Various members of the bands that are on the bill plus their hangers-on, who are slumped on couches, are all unceremoniously kicked out to make way for Diddy and company. Busboys replenish the room with the three-foot-high bottles of vodka that are being served at the party, and the color of the wristbands that allows people entrance into the room is swiftly changed from yellow to white. This quick switch transforms bearers of the former wristband from VIPs to hoi polloi in the blink of an eye. A few moments after Diddy and his posse have settled in, Thomas leaves his door post, replaces his yellow wristband with a white one, and enters the VIP room.

This part of the club is a surreal affair: the VIP room is a raised area that overlooks the dance floor and has been decorated with a "trailer trash" theme. An old Airstream trailer has been converted into a bar, a white picket fence encircles the room, with lawn chairs, pink flamingos and a barbeque grill completing the lower-middle-class design scheme. The room has a separate DJ, and as Thomas enters the space a robotic electro dance song is playing. Thomas looks over in the direction of the Airstream and sees Timbaland sitting on an aluminum, plastic-cushioned love seat. In front of him, a female member of Diddy's posse is writhing like a harem dancer—faster than the beat of the music—as if performing some kind of bizarre private dance for him. Timbaland doesn't react and just stares ahead, as if the woman is invisible.

As the song's electronic belches gurgle gently to an end and segue into a remix of Fischerspooner's "Emerge," Thomas runs into Felix da Housecat, Leigh, and Geo. Geo is wearing super-short little boy Adidas running shorts and a tank top that he's sliced down nearly to his navel. This ensemble, combined with his foppish mop top, makes him look like a nineteenth-century street urchin who's been time-warped into a twenty-first-century grammar school gym class. Leigh picks up one of the outsized vodka bottles and helps raise it to Geo's lips. After a long slug, he uproots one of the plastic flamingos, turns to Thomas, and yanks on the sleeve of his *Golden Girls*/Puerto Rican housewife jacket. "Thomas! I got you a present for being such an awesome door bitch!"

Felix walks over and grabs Geo's arm. "Hey, you want to meet Diddy?"

"Sure, why not?" Geo says, sticking the flamingo back into the Astroturf that covers the floor. "Diddy, this is my man Geo. He does a really awesome party in New York called MisShapes. He's going to be DJing in this room in a little while." Diddy, who is brandishing a glass of tequila, looks Geo up and down like a searchlight. *Oh lord, what is Diddy going to think of him? Geo couldn't look any gayer,* Thomas says to himself, forgetting for a moment the irony of his own Latina Bea Arthur persona. "Hey, Geo, nice to meet you," Diddy shakes his hand while continuing to study Geo's barely-there outfit. "So, do you like hip-hop?" Without missing a beat Geo responds, "I *am* hip-hop!" Diddy bursts out laughing. "I love this man, get him a drink right now!" Within seconds, a team of cocktail servers appears bearing shots of tequila for everyone.

After Thomas downs his shot, he goes out into the main room and surveys the crowd of people on the dance floor. As he's winding his way through the crowd, he bumps into two friends—Sia Michel, the editor-in-chief of *Spin,* and Tricia Romano, a columnist for *The Village Voice.* "This is so surreal!" Sia tells Thomas. The trio stands there together for a few moments laughing, as Tricia takes photos of the crowd with her digital camera. At this point, people aren't so much dancing as they are standing in front of the DJ booth—which is raised only a few feet off the ground—and behaving as if the DJ were a rock star. The kids wave their arms, bang their heads, and hoot and holler as if they are at a heavy metal gig fifteen or twenty years ago. As he moves across the room, Thomas bumps into Larry Tee. "I love this party, it's the perfect mix of kids who like indie rock and techno," the New York DJ enthuses. "And the predictable kids who would feel more at home in Ibiza aren't really here."

The DJ who is spinning at the moment is DJ Hell, a notoriously aloof German tastemaker who is so famous in his hometown of Berlin, he can barely walk down the street. Hell, who founded Gigolo Records, is credited with starting the underground electro dance music craze and is currently appeasing the crowd at the Pawn Shop with a hard-as-nails electronic set. Suddenly Diddy appears in the DJ booth and begins jumping up and down. Not expecting this uber-celeb intrusion, Hell at first seems to have a hard time keeping his cool. "I can't tell if he's weirded out in a good way or a bad way," Thomas shouts into Larry's ear. "This is very exciting," Larry replies. "It's sort of like the highbrow and lowbrow of the music world colliding!"

Hell exits the DJ booth and Felix da Housecat takes over the reigns. As photographers form a gauntlet in front of the DJ booth, someone has inexplicably handed Diddy a bullhorn. "Everybody say 'ho-ohh'!" Diddy bellows into the bullhorn. "Let's hear it for Feeelix!" Felix starts laughing as the crowd is slowly being whipped into a frenzy. Hundreds of kids begin holding up their cell phones to take pictures, much like the audiences who held up their lighters to salute rock stars at concerts in the 'eighties. "Everyone say 'ho-ooohooh'!"

Hell returns to the DJ booth and begins tag-team DJing with Felix, as Diddy continues his surreal cheerleader act. In the middle of the electro-techno speed rush, one of the digital demons drops Marilyn Manson's "The Beautiful People" into the mix and the tribal drums and machine gun guitars drive the crowd berserk. Thomas retreats from the flailing mass of club crawlers and wanders back into a courtyard area of the venue. The MisShapes have finished their DJ set, and Leigh and Greg have taken to ecstatically dancing on top of a pool table. "You can't dance up there!" the manager screams, and tries to tip over the table in an attempt to send the happy-go-lucky hoofers toppling to the floor.

Thomas walks into another room and finds Geo passed out on a couch, sleeping like a baby. Suddenly, a fashionably dressed blonde woman staggers over to the couch and plops down right on top of the slumbering small fry. "Hey Tricia!" she bellows drunkenly to Tricia Romano. "Get a load of this! Com'ere and take my picture!"

"Get off of my client right now!" Thomas screams at her. "You're crushing him!"

"Hey, calm down lady, I'm just trying to have a little fun," she slurs back at him. "Love the jacket. You get that from the Goodwill shop offa Lincoln Road?"

"No, it's Adidas, and get off my friend right now. I'm not asking you, I'm telling you," Thomas says angrily, making a move for her. "It's considered rude to *sit on top* of people without their consent, okay?" The woman slides off of Geo, who remains sleeping through the whole altercation. *How could some-one sleep through an ordeal like that?* Thomas thinks. The answer comes when he turns around and sees Leigh and Greg dragging one of the giant vodka bottles into the room. "Where's Geo?" Leigh asks. "We thought he might want a little pick-me-up." Exhausted, Thomas throws himself down on the couch next to Geo, unzips his ironic Bea Arthur jacket, and grabs a clean plastic cup from a nearby dispenser. "I think Geo may have reached his quota," Thomas says, as he holds his cup out to Leigh. "But 'Dorothy' could definitely use a little nip."

In March 2004, a spectacle rained down on New York that has now come to be known as the Week of Courtney Love. From Courtney flashing her breasts on *Late Night with David Letter-man,* to having the same breasts suckled in front of a McDon-ald's, to her performance in an "Eat My Fuck" T-shirt dress at the Bowery Ballroom, the raucous, raunchy action was non-stop . . . and every computer and TV screen from Chattanooga to Calcutta was tuned in to her campaign of rock 'n' roll ter-rorism. Her antics may have caused some wincing, but there was a seductive quality to her mayhem as well. Even the stoic Gray Lady cautiously flirted with the punk provocateur: "Per-haps Courtney Love's Wednesday should be dipped in gold and mounted on the wall at the Rock and Roll Hall of Fame, as a classic specimen of punk rock misbehavior," *The New York Times* mused. The Wednesday in question—her surprise con-

cert with her band The Chelsea at a club called Plaid—was the
gin-soaked maraschino cherry on top of the overly frosted En-
tenmann's cake—and Thomas was at the ropes to see it all.

"I've been a huge fan of Courtney's since *Pretty on the Inside*
came out in 1991," Thomas enthuses. "And I was very excited
to be doing the door to that special performance." Not only was
Thomas the doorman to this exclusive concert, but he was also
instrumental in helping spread the word to the right people: he
and the promoters leaked word of Courtney's scheduled appearance to their contacts one day before the show. "Courtney and
her band members showed up at Plaid in a limo after taking in
sets by Jet and The Vines at Irving Plaza. After a half hour she
came back outside with a few friends and they went into the
limo for about ten minutes, so she could 'look for a pair of
shoes' that she wanted to wear," Thomas recalls. "She was definitely high, but she was very professional, and the club's staff
and I enjoyed working with her throughout the night." After
her alleged wardrobe change in the limo, Courtney and her
band took the stage for what is considered one of the most legendary New York rock gigs of the 'noughties. Between new and
old songs, the disheveled diva called out beverage requests
("Get the Jameson, get the Cristal!"), passed the virtual hat
("Get me all the money in the bank so I can get my daughter
back."), and expressed gratitude ("Thanks for not raping me.
That's the first time that hasn't happened in ten years!").

"I snuck away from my post at the door so I could catch
some of the show," Thomas remembers excitedly. "She was

singing 'Malibu,' and the room was completely packed—
people standing on couches, chairs, everything. Courtney was
both completely on and all over the map . . . it was one of the
most spontaneous performances I've ever seen. You felt as if
anything could happen." And something did happen. Courtney flung a mike stand down on the stage, causing the metal
rod to jet out into the audience and hit someone in the head.

"I was back outside at the door and suddenly this guy comes
out with blood running down his face, and I was, like, 'Oh my
god, what happened? We need to call an ambulance!' But before we could do that, a cop appeared out of nowhere and said
'I'll take care of that.' He followed the man into the club. A few
moments later, one of the security guards popped his head out
of the club and told me that the guy wanted to press charges
against Courtney."

Word spread through the club and after a few journalists
made some cell phone calls, photographers from the Associated
Press, Reuters, and the *New York Post*, began showing up in
front of the club. "Thirty minutes later a bunch of cop cars,
with sirens blaring and lights spinning, pulled up around the
corner where the side entrance of the club was. It became evi-
dent that they were planning on taking Courtney away from
the side of the club," says Thomas. "All of the photographers
ran over to the other entrance when the cop cars pulled up. But
then all of a sudden my entrance opens and a woman with a
parka draped over her shoulders and with the hood pulled
down over her face came out escorted by two policemen. When

she walked by me I noticed that her wrists were in handcuffs and that it was Courtney. They led her into an unmarked car. One photographer did get wise to the situation and ran over and snapped her photo while she was sitting in the front seat of the car. But the other photographers were fooled by the decoy set by the police. Because the club had such a good relationship with the law, they were able to negotiate that and spare Courtney harassment by the paparazzi." Courtney spent the night in jail and was later ordered by Manhattan Criminal Court to cover the man's medical expenses.

8 .

You step the stage and take control.

—THE FAINT

It was four A.M., on a wet night in New York in the fall of 1987, when a drag queen named Princess Myra was stumbling up Twenty-third Street in terror. An androgynous man dressed in a London schoolboy uniform, with a full face of makeup, and the front half of his head shaved—was a few yards behind her in hot pursuit. "What's wrong, bitch? Having a hard time walking in those heels?" Kenny Kenny, who was the doorperson for a club called Savage at the time, shrieked tauntingly. "You fuckin' drunken whore!" Like the marauding snakehead fish that were believed to be able to leave the water and walk on land in search of prey, Kenny Kenny had left the confines of the club's ropes. "I was one doorman who would leave my post at the door," Kenny says of his particular style of door whoring, as he recalls that evening. "She had given me a hard time because I made her pay five dollars to get in, and when she was leaving she called me a baldheaded drunk. Whenever this sort of thing happened, I would follow people and berate them, terrorize them. I think the way I dealt with people back then was by really lashing out at them."

Closing the guest list without warning. Interrogating club-goers as if they were criminals. Verbal tongue-lashings. Merciless outfit critiques. Icy glares. Mind games. These are just some of the various door bitch antics that are employed outside clubs on a nightly basis. "I will admit that I have an overwhelming need for control," says Thomas. "And I have a repertoire of tactics and announcements which I use to maintain that control while working at the door."

For example, if Thomas tells certain clubgoers that they will need to wait or that they are not on the list, these individuals may proceed to appeal to every other person who is working the door in the hopes of bypassing Thomas's decision or instructions. When this happen, Thomas tells them: "I appreciate you taking the time to interview my entire staff, but you *still* have to wait in line." Then there are others who just want to look inside the club quickly for "a friend who might be in there." Other variants include: "I have my friend's cell phone/car keys/apartment keys/lifesaving medication, and I need to get in there and give it to him/her." Thomas will then say to them, "This is a nightclub, not a supermarket—do you see any oranges inside?" It may seem cruel, but Thomas notes "I know they are lying and will probably end up staying inside for at least an hour."

Because the nightlife world often resembles a giant playground—complete with bratty adolescent behavior, temper tantrums, childlike selfishness, and lots of "candy"—immature acts that most adults would not manifest during daylight hours can become rampant once the sun goes down. Even though a good doorman strives to be above this kind of behavior, he is certainly not immune to stooping to the level of a typically mouthy patron. "It was typical schoolyard stuff, where you felt like you had to say it or you would disintegrate," explains Kenny of his earlier days as a doorman. "People still come up to me and tell me things I said years ago and I have no recollection of them." According to someone who claims to remember, one night, while tending the door to the Copacabana—a spectacular monthly party thrown by Susanne Bartsch during the early nineties—Kenny was reading a note. Someone who was outside the ropes tried to get his attention by asking him, "What are you reading, Kenny?"

"It's a letter from an admirer!" Kenny barked imperiously. "How *dare* you interrupt me!"

"Working at those doors, I developed this mindset that I was allowed to say or do anything," says Kenny, who has been working as a doorman in New York since 1987. "Those were very crazy times." His claim of not remembering certain incidents suggests that he often went into a fugue state—a pathological amnesiac condition, during which someone is apparently conscious of one's actions but has no memory of them afterwards. Of course, there are other explanations. "You have to remember, sometimes I was drunk," the now-sober Kenny admits. "Also, I've seen so many things, it's too much to remember." There are glimmers of recollection that do emerge, however. "One thing I do remember is when I would be told by a club owner to stop the guest list, because the club was too full. So I would shout "There is no guest list tonight!" at anyone who insisted they were on the list. There was a house music song in the 'nineties that was inspired by me, where someone is trying—and failing—to imitate my voice: 'Miss Thing, there is no guest list toniiight!' It truly was a horrible song."

One notorious Kenny Kenny story involves two East Village performance artists who arrived at the door of the club called The World, where Kenny guarded the ropes in the early 'nineties. "We had an invitation that admitted two people for free, all night long," explains one of the victims. "And Kenny looked at it and said belligerently 'This invitation is no longer valid,' and I said 'Says who? That makes no sense,' and Kenny replied viciously, 'Says me. And *I'm* invalidating it!' and then he proceeded to rip up the invitation right in front of my face. He had long, red fingernails, which resembled talons, and he was wearing a blue fun fur shawl, except there was nothing fun about him. He looked like one of the clawed beasts from that children's book *Where the Wild Things Are*. The whole experience was very unsettling. But it got worse than that.

"A week later I was hanging out at this notorious East Village after-hours club called Save the Robots—people would go there after places like The World and Tunnel closed and do drugs and drink, because, somehow, the bar was still able to serve booze until the sun came up—and longer. Kenny was there and he was very drunk. He was wearing a bizarre hair net, and there was so much makeup on his face it was flaking off in huge chunks, like the flesh of a leper. He was also wearing a black vinyl corset and a cape. It was a very bride of Satan kind of look. He didn't remember me and tried to hand me an invitation to a party he was doing the door to and I snapped at him. 'Why bother giving me an invitation to some club you won't let me into, you has-been!' Kenny was livid. He started talking to himself saying things like '*Has-bean?* Did you hear what he called me? He called me a has-bean,' and his gin and tonic was sloshing around and spilling everywhere. Then he came very close to me and looked me straight in the eye—I still get chills when I think about it—and said in an ominous tone, starting out slowly, and then quickly, 'Let me get a good look at your face . . . I want to remember you so that I will NEVER LET YOU INTO ONE OF MY PARTIES EVER AGAIN!' And then he reached up and clawed at me with his scarlet talons and scratched my chest and shrieked 'I'm going to BEAT YOU DOWN!' As I was backing away, I saw him go over to a huge man—possibly a drug dealer—and say 'See that person over there? He called me a has-bean. Do me a favor and BEAT HIM DOWN!' At this point I ran for the nearest exit and got the hell out of there. After that, every time I saw a club invitation that said "Door: Kenny Kenny," my blood ran cold.

When he started working at the Copa, I went in drag and not only did he not recognize me, he let me in right away. It was the perfect disguise."

"I'm a little bit different than someone like Kenny Kenny, I'm not out there to fuck with people or ruin anyone's night. It's bad karma," insists Thomas, despite the fact that he has said admiringly of the prototypal doorman: "Kenny Kenny is ground zero for a lot of things you see me doing." Everything would include mean-spirited put-downs about people's attire. "I was doing the door to a benefit—for what, I can't remember—at a place called Delancey one night, and this hipster girl wanted to get in without paying," Thomas recalls. "I said 'this is a benefit' and she said to her friend 'This guy's a dick! Let's get out of here.' She was wearing a denim skirt, cowboy boots, and a camouflage jacket. As she was leaving, I said 'Just so you know, camo is the new silver and you should know that already.' I mean, hello? Camouflage was *so* two seasons ago by that point."

There is also good old-fashioned, point-blank rudeness. When people are overly persistent about getting in, even when they are told that it's guest list only, Thomas will bark at them, "You heard what I said—is English your second language?" Sometimes the rudeness becomes physical. "One night Thomas was doing the door to an intimate party for a fashion designer named Zaldy, which was held at the Soho Grand Hotel," a close friend of Thomas's relates. "They had a small patch of red carpet—a red doormat basically—in front of the entrance to a tiny room, with three photographers stationed in front of it. But they were like photographers for Web sites that no one has ever heard of, it's not like they were shooting for *Vogue* or *The New York Times*. Thomas got to decide who would be photographed and who wasn't worth wasting precious film on. Even though I am a well-known writer who often gets seated in the front row at fashion shows—and have known Thomas for ten years—he deemed me unworthy of a photo op. I was with this guy, Lee Carter, who does a fashion site called hintmag.com, and Thomas pushed me as hard as he could out of the way and grabbed Lee, saying to me 'You—go. I need Lee.' It was very rude and almost ended our friendship. And it makes you wonder what kind of misdirected hostility these types have that leads them to choose the doorman profession."

"What can I say? Nightlife is a tough business," Thomas says in response to this story. "And New York is a tough town. I think that most of the time I'm very fair and very professional, but the arena of the velvet ropes can sometimes be as brutal as Ancient Roman-style justice or the Spanish Inquisition. There is no law in the arena. Sometimes there's going to be some casualities and bruised egos. It's not all fabulousness, air kisses, and drink tickets all the time."

Thomas may be one of New York's most prominent door bitches, but you don't need a degree in nightclubbing to know that there have been others before him—and that he certainly isn't the first to employ an arsenal of door bitch antics to keep the seething masses under control. Some of doormen that precede him—like Kenny Kenny—are still working doors around town, while others are retired from the ropes and are as seemingly tangible as dry ice smoke on a dance floor of yore, like the man who worked at what is widely considered to be "the greatest club of all time . . ."

In the beginning, Steve Rubell created Studio 54 and the door scene. Steve said, "Let there be velvet ropes and disco and quaaludes. Let there be Bianca and Andy and Truman and Disco Sally. Let there be the Man in the Moon with the Silver Coke Spoon. But those who seek entry into Paradise wearing polyester shall be cast into the fiery lake . . . also known as the club Xenon."

"Steve runs Studio 54 like his living room. He only lets in people he likes," Andy Warhol said, back in the day. "He likes beautiful girls, beautiful boys, stars, society, and press. He wants a balance, 'a tossed salad.' " Steve Rubell invented door bitch antics. His notorious behavior at the velvet ropes ranged from asking people to remove all their clothes, separating engaged couples by only letting the man in, burning holes in polyester lapels, and hurling insults at the decidedly unfabulous. But he was not alone in this endeavor.

"When someone came to the door, if they had incredible energy or if I knew they were going to bring something visually to the party, that would get them in," says Marc Benecke, the man who worked Studio 54's ropes with Rubell, starting on the club's first night in April 1977. "It didn't matter if you worked in a McDonald's or you worked at Dior—it was about the individual and what you brought to the forefront." Marc was only nineteen when he was asked to guard the gates of the newcomer to New York's quickly growing discothèque scene. Even though he had been considering a job in law or politics, he realized immediately that he had a special knack for manning the ropes. But rather than relying on the door bitch antics that Rubell employed, Marc would focus on the people in the crowd that he knew would get in and ignored everyone else. "I was very aloof while I was at the door, that was my way of coping with it. I'm sure I came off as arrogant," Marc says. "One thing I didn't like was when people tried too hard. I didn't like gimmicks. Obviously I let a lot of out-rageous and flamboyant people in because they brought a lot to the mix, but if I sensed that some-one had put on a costume just so they could get in, that didn't fly with me." Marc admits that he wasn't always right in his decisions, such as when he refused entry to Disco Sally—Studio's famed septuagenarian party girl—during the club's early days. "I didn't let her in the first four or five times she came," Marc remembers. "But Steve finally let her in; he saw something I didn't see . . . and, of

THE MYTHS OF STUDIO 54

Tall tales from New York's most legendary night-club are still told to-day; but how many of them are actually true? 54's famed doorman, Marc Benecke, sorts out the myths and the realities.

MYTH: Marc Benecke didn't let Cher into Studio. Celebrity wasn't a guarantee for en-trance at Studio, with Cher be-ing one of the renowned rejects. "But I'm Cher!" the diva allegedly said. "I know who you are and you're still not getting in," was Marc's infa-mous reply.

REALITY: "It's not true!" says Marc. "And I actually became very friendly with Cher later on. I have no idea how that rumor got started."

MYTH: The disco group Chic didn't get in. Nile Rodgers and Bernard Edwards of Chic had been invited by Grace Jones, but Marc wouldn't let them in. Furious, they went home and

Continued

wrote a song about their door ordeal that went "ahhh, fuck off!" They later changed the lyrics to "ahhh, freak out!" and the song "Le Freak" sold over six million copies.

REALITY: "It's true," Marc says with slight embarrassment. "I had plenty of moments at the ropes when I just did things because I felt like it. But they made millions off that song, so they certainly had the last laugh!"

MYTH: A man who was turned away at the door tried to get into Studio by sliding down an air shaft. He got stuck in the shaft and died. "It smelled like a cat had died," said Baird Jones, who worked at Studio. "He was in black tie."

REALITY: "Yes, someone did get stuck in the air vent, but he didn't die," Marc says, sighing at the mention of this oft-repeated gossip. "They were able to get him out on that night."

Continued

course, she became an important part of the show."

Studio closed in 1980 in the wake of a tax evasion scandal that resulted in Rubell and his partner Ian Schrager being sent to prison. They reopened in 1981 and Marc worked the ropes for the first six months, but the club never regained its original magic. "They didn't need me out there anymore," he says. After a couple of years of promoting parties inside Studio, Marc left for Los Angeles to pursue other ventures. "I worked the door at a club called Peanuts, on Santa Monica Boulevard," Marc recalls. "The door policy was definitely more democratic than it was at Studio. I had this feeling of going from the pinnacle—Studio— to a club where people mostly waited politely in line to get in, but it was okay. It was part of my whole post-Studio, L.A. learning experience." After Peanuts, Marc went back to school and then embarked on a career of bar and club management, including working as manager and food and beverage director for many Ian Schrager hotels, such as The Clift in San Francisco and the Shore Club in Miami. Marc may have moved on, but the style of working the door that he and Rubell pioneered continues to be the template today.

"I do feel responsible for the technique of the way doors are done now, whether that's a good or bad thing . . . but in today's society, I don't think it's necessary to do the door the way it used to be done," Marc says. "Unless it's an exclusive event—like Madonna DJing at a small venue for example—I think that these days doormen are hitting people over the head with a sledgehammer, when all they need is a tiny little thumbtack. In L.A., at places like The Tattoo Club in Beverly Hills, I've seen doormen rip up guest lists or artificially hold people outside for no reason, and I think, 'Why are they being such idiots at the door? There's no reason for it.' I've heard so many club owners say, 'We're going to re-create Studio,' and I always think of a quote about 54 that was in *The Village Voice*: 'You can't reheat soufflé.' That's the best way of putting it."

Marc still has fond memories of that soufflé and of those days in general. "Studio was closed on Monday nights, but Xenon was open—and that club was actually good on those nights," Marc says of Studio's déclassé competitor. When he realizes what he's just said out loud, he presses his hands together in a prayer pose and gazes heavenward. "Please forgive me for saying that, Steve!"

MYTH: Jackie O. was a Studio 54 regular.

REALITY: "When journalists write generalized articles about Studio, Jackie's name is often mentioned in the lineup of famous attendees," Marc notes. "To my knowledge—and I was at the door every night from day one—Jackie O. never came to Studio. We tried to get her to go many times, but she never went."

MYTH: After Bianca Jagger rode into Studio on a white horse on her birthday—one week after the club opened—there was never a dull moment.

REALITY: "That is basically true, and the Bianca party definitely put Studio on the map," Marc confirms. "There were calmer nights, like Tuesdays, when the door scene was less chaotic, less stressful. But the party was still pumping inside."

* * *

It's July 2005, another club opening night in New York, and Kenny Kenny is daintily stepping out into the street to survey the seemingly endless lineup outside of Area 10018. "This has got to end soon; this is going on forever," Kenny says. "Where did I leave my can of Red Bull?" He has been hired as the door-person for this new party, in charge of the usual: who gets in for free, who pays a discount, and who pays full price. "If this was a night in the 'eighties, everyone would be out in the street in a mob and I would be picking and choosing," Kenny says with a hint of wistfulness in his voice. "Look how orderly everyone is lined up—where's the fun?" Tonight Kenny is wearing trousers that are cropped, minishorts-length on one leg, reveal-ing a fishnet stockinged leg. Half of a Dali-style mustache graces his upper lip and a metal-sequined disc is attached to the front of his shaved head. His half man, half woman ensem-ble seems to draw inspiration from Dadaist performance cos-tumes circa 1918. Only the very bold or those beckoned by Kenny forgo the long line and enter past the rope that Kenny lifts. The singer Rufus Wainwright shows up stag and he and his abundance of exposed chest hair are swiftly admitted. "Make way for Rufus," Kenny announces cheerfully, his sinis-ter, wicked queen delivery of yesteryear curiously absent. When Kenny informs a pair of young men of the fifteen-dollar admission, one of them huffily inquires about a student dis-count. In the old days Kenny would have belched volcanic vitriol, leaving a pile of lifeless, Pompeii-like ashes where the boy once stood. Instead he chides the disagreeable student with the demeanor of a strict, yet loving—and very surreal—kindergarten teacher. "You can't pay fifteen dollars, darling? How about ten dollars? Well now, you didn't expect to get in for free, did you?" The boy grimaces. Kenny gives him and his friend five-dollar discounts. He then summons a brood of pixieish goth girls over to his station. "Let's get some female cuties in here," he says to Brandon, his door partner for the evening. "But we're cute too!" complains a young man sporting a Tin-Tin hairdo and a camouflage Abercrombie tank top, who is standing with a male friend. "Yes dear, you're cute too," Kenny says charitably. "And I'll let you in next, right after I take care of the girls."

What has happened to Kenny Kenny? Where is the acid-tongued hellhound who single-handedly turned door scenes in New York into terrifying, sadistic rituals? "I was channeling the devil in those days—I blame him. I've had my exorcism and I'm fine now," a repentant Kenny jokes. "I'm not the door-person I was, which is good. I try to be nice to everyone now so I don't go home all wound up and hating myself. Back in the late 'eighties and early 'nineties people expected me to act that way—it was part of the show. People loved to hate me, but at least I gave drama and added some excitement. Plus, back then people were more high maintenance . . . everyone felt like a star, and, really, someone had to discipline the children." Reflecting further back on those days, Kenny says he was "really

channeling Shiva—the Hindu god who creates and destroys—
in his most ferocious form, but underneath the fury was com-
passion. In the end it all got the better of me and I developed
chronic fatigue syndrome, and Shiva, or the universe, told me
it was time to chill out and try a new way, a new energy."

Some may view such mystical rhetoric as pretentious, but
Kenny could do worse than a Shiva analogy—after all, he was
working to create great parties while simultaneously destroying egos. As Kenny's acolyte, Thomas certainly has similar
Shiva-like qualities. But what really makes a door bitch such a
bitch? Aside from the vast and hectic demands of the job, what
psychological factors fuel the door bitches' antics? With
Thomas, body issues, residual middle-class anger, and paranoia
about the sincerity of friends are some of the culprits; but what
is the genesis of Kenny's "caustic, witty tongue"?

"I grew up on the mean streets of a small village in Ireland,
near the north," Kenny relates. "Where it was 'fight or flight'.
There was nowhere to run, so I fought. Because I was an openly
effeminate kid in this provincial village, I was ostracized to the
point where it was ridiculous . . . I could not walk down the
street without being berated and called all sorts of names. So I
had to learn how to defend myself with my tongue, with
words. We Irish are quite good with words, and we have a way
with words that I find quite poetic. We also have a rebellious
spirit—that's something that's inbred in us." Kenny's home
village, Cootehill, is located in Cavan County in the divided
Province of Ulster right on the border of Northern Ireland and

the Republic of Ireland. It's a county that was pivotal in the early days of Irish independence and is known for its political tension.

"My grandfather campaigned for Arthur Griffin—a founder of the Sinn Fein movement which was associated with the IRA—from the house that I was born in. Even though my grandfather had nonviolent political views, he was put in a British prison camp for a few years. An apology can never make up for what the English did to the Irish. I grew up with an old battle cry, 'Ireland unfree shall never be at peace!' I think I got a little bit of that fighting spirit from my grandfather . . . he was the one person who was supportive of me."

Kenny is not out to make excuses for his excessive behavior at the velvet ropes, but to a certain extent he does acknowledge the factor of Irish rage from his childhood. "I'm sure, at the doors of clubs I've worked at, if I perceived that people were coming for me or attacking me, my nature was to give worse than I was getting. When I started doing doors in 1987, I just thought that was how you had to be . . . I didn't know there was another way. Now I realize there is another way." For a clearer answer on where this style of ruthless velvet ropes management developed, one need only look to one geographic location: London. "I saw how the door people were behaving in London in the early 'eighties and I looked to them as mentors," says Kenny. "Dysfunctional mentors."

Kenny remembers one incident where he was on the receiving end of British door bitchery. "I went to the famous disco

Heaven, on gay night, with a girl who was dressed like a boy, and I was dressed in a suit with my hair slicked back, lots of makeup, very androgynous. The club's notorious doorgirl—who was working a dominatrix kind of look—starting barking at us, 'Separate! Separate! I want to see what's going on here!' She thought we were holding hands, that we were lovers, and her job that night was to keep the straight people out . . . and she decided we were straight and said 'No. Go!' and pointed for us to leave. So I lashed out at her and said 'Not only am I not allowed to be gay in my own country, now I'm not even allowed to be gay in this fucking country!' And then the door bitch changed her mind, which for me is a very doorperson thing, it's something I do all the time. I test people, and it just shows you that door people are just trying to figure it out sometimes—it's not always black and white."

These days Kenny likes to spend much of his time traveling around the world, taking photos, and promoting and hosting parties—he is in "semiretirement" from door whoring. "I *hate* doing doors. I think I did it when there was a certain amount of fun in it, but I don't like doing them anymore. I think they're hideous things . . . hideous squares of bad energy. Unless everybody gets in, I don't like working the door."

They arrive in droves, emboldened with the kind of aggressive chutzpah that German soldiers possessed when they marched into Paris. Marc Jacobs bags swing menacingly like pistols and

Gucci perfume hangs in the air like nerve gas, as this phalanx of ersatz Carries, Samanthas, and Mirandas halt before the velvet ropes. They have come to the Roxy to do what these sort of girls do when they are granted entrance into this sort of disco: terrorize the bartenders with inappropriate drink orders, noisily invade the dance floor, and hunt for potential captives. Their quarry: attractive, amusing, nonthreatening men. Gays.

"All twenty of you are together?!" Derek Neen asks incredulously. "I'm sorry but tonight is for the boys. I really can't let you in." Derek lifts the rope that holds waiting guests at bay, while a security team cohort lifts another rope that will allow the girlish junta to pass momentarily through the box—but only so they can exit onto the sidewalk from whence they came. The mob emits a series of disappointed bleats as they clip-clop past the ropes in their Manolo- and Jimmy Choo-shod feet. In the blink of an eye, the group has been transformed from a squadron of weekend warriors to herded barnyard animals. "There are other places you can go," Derek shouts over the din, the velvet rope held aloft. "There are plenty of straight clubs that are more than happy to welcome the ladies."

Derek has been the doorman for the Roxy's Saturday night gay party for fifteen years. The forty-five-year-old Canadian also runs the ropes on the club's nongay Friday nights, which are often devoted to grand R & B music events. That night's predominantly black crowd brings to the club a retro form of Harlem sophistication—men in zoot suits and fedoras, women in cocktail dresses and chinchilla stoles—which is in marked contrast to the Saturday night gay crowd's sausage casing–tight tees and jeans, and various stages of ill-advised transvestism. In order to preserve the gay male vibe of this long-running party, one of Derek's chores is to limit the number of women entering the club. "Tonight is only for the boys, but I might let you in if you can come up with a good defense," Derek, wearing a foxlike smile, tells two women.

"We came all the way from Long Island!" they plead.

"Long Island?!" Derek affects alarm. "Do you have your visas with you?" Stunned by this humorous sting of Manhattan jingoism, the girls fall silent. Derek dives directly into interrogation mode. "Did you know it was a gay night? What other clubs do you go to? Why did you come here?"

"My mom thinks I'm gay!" one girl blurts out, as if she is cracking under the pressure.

"Will you make out with another girl if I let you in?" Derek asks pointedly. The girl grimaces. Derek sends them packing. When another group of girls show up and are identified as Canadians by their accents, Derek subjects them to a pop quiz concerning their country's history. "Who was the first prime minister of Canada?" Derek asks. "And who was the head of the Metis?" When the girls answer all of the questions correctly, Derek opens the ropes for them and the group bobbles excitedly into the club like winners on *Jeopardy*. "You're *so* entertaining!" trills a gay man waiting in line, who is wearing a T-shirt that says DEFINE "GIRLFRIEND."

"I like to keep things interesting for people who are waiting near the front of the line, because they want to see things like that—it's show business," Derek is fond of saying. "Whether I'm quizzing people or telling jokes or chatting up stars, it's a bit like being on stage . . . and also my job as a doorman is essentially my only 'going-out' life, so I do a lot of socializing in front of the club. I could be chatting with someone like John Norris from MTV or Carson from *Queer Eye* or minor or major European aristocracy, and I'll talk just loud enough so the people who are waiting in line can get in on it, because I don't want them to feel excluded . . . and the people I'm speaking to understand that, they know it's a stage—they know they're supposed to be on."

Later on that night Hollywood fashion stylist Philip Bloch arrives, stands in front of the roped entrance reserved for VIPs, and props himself up on the stanchions, waiting to be noticed. He is wearing a sleeveless mesh athletic shirt and a cocky expression that says "Hello? Here I am!" As Derek greets him warmly, the boys at the front of the line aim a rapid-fire series of questions at Philip concerning his recent E! channel appearances. "So Philip, how do these boys look? What's the style diagnosis?" Philip makes a sour lemon face and then waves dismissively in their direction. "I'm off duty tonight," he says, before filling Derek in on his recent trip to Australia, much to the waiting boys' delight.

Whereas Kenny's early velvet rope days resembled Grand Guignol and Thomas's door bitchery is often an exercise in twenty-first-century efficiency, Derek's door-side manner is

TOP 10 REASONS THE DOOR BITCH GIVES FOR NOT LETTING YOU IN

Thomas and his door bitch brethren have a mental list of reasons for why you're not getting in. Sometimes they bend the truth and other times they're brutally frank. Here are the most popular decrees and what they actually mean.

WHAT THE DOOR BITCH SAYS: "Sorry, it's guest list only/a private party tonight."

WHAT IT REALLY MEANS: "You're kidding right? Did you really think I'd let you in dressed like *that*?"

WHAT THE DOOR BITCH SAYS: "The club is full to capacity; you're going to have to wait awhile."

WHAT IT REALLY MEANS: "This club is over and tired and

Continued

something akin to a vaudeville act. At his Tuesday night door gig, Beige—a long-running gay party at Bowery Bar—Derek tosses off corny one-liners as he edits a nonstop parade of fashionistas, hair and makeup artists, NYU students, and nightlife diehards, with the latter receiving a sly "good morning!" from him as they stride up at midnight. Women attired as if they're female female impersonators enter undeterred, while other ladies, who arrive on the arms of men who are in the practice of posing as gay in order to secure entry, are stopped. "Are you straight?" Derek asks a preppie-looking man who has shown up with a slender blonde. "No, I have a husband but he's in Budapest," the man replies. Derek emits a stagey Bronx cheer. "Budapest? That was no husband! If you have to pay for it, he's not a real husband!" Derek cracks. Later, a Russian girl with a heavy accent arrives with two men, but sans ID. DADDY'S GIRL is printed across her T-shirt in gold letters. "But I'm twenty-seven," she insists.

"So where's Daddy?" Derek asks.

"Daddy's in Istanbul. He sells airplanes."

"Sounds like Russian mafia to me! What do you do for a living?" he asks.

"I'm studying liberal arts at the New School," she explains.

"What? You're still in school at twenty-seven? Sounds more like the *Nude* School—that strip joint out in Brighton Beach!" Derek says, channeling Jackie Mason.

As the evening progresses, gaggles of friends and acquaintances have gathered in front of the door, filling Derek in on the details of recent trips to Paris, photo shoot gossip, relationship drama, and fashion bulletins. There is a sense that the real party is happening outside—in Derek's honor—rather than inside. At around one A.M. elderly Andy Warhol factory legend, Taylor Meade, hobbles up the front steps with his cane, his characteristic goofy grin lighting up the night. "Taylor!" Derek exclaims, and the entire crowd of lingerers and line-waiters bursts into applause and cheers. Taylor raises his cane above his head and basks in the glory. "Taylor has been coming here for eleven years and he always drinks for free," Derek tells a friend. "And I even have the young people here trained to receive him in a manner that befits an icon. Everyone knows Taylor."

Derek hails from a small city in British Columbia called Kamloops (First Nations word

currently only one-third full . . . so we need to have a crowd waiting outside so people will think it's hot again." (Note: Sometimes the doorman is telling the truth and there are actually people duct-taped to the ceiling because the space is so jam-packed.)

WHAT THE DOOR BITCH SAYS: "This invitation is no longer valid. You'll need to pay ten dollars each."

WHAT IT REALLY MEANS: "The club promoter/owner realized that they distributed too many freebie invites, and now they need to make some money."

WHAT THE DOOR BITCH SAYS: "There is no guest list tonight."

WHAT IT REALLY MEANS: "This is the decision made by the greedy owner who is trying to dick over the promoters. The promoters get paid based on the number of people who show up from their guest lists, so the owner has decided he wants a bigger cut for himself

Continued

and does this by eliminating the guest list."

WHAT THE DOOR BITCH SAYS: "This isn't a supermarket, it's a nightclub. There is no browsing."

WHAT IT REALLY MEANS: "You're not getting in by using some lame excuse about your friend waiting for you inside."

WHAT THE DOOR BITCH SAYS: "You guys look really cute, in fact you're all really gorgeous."

WHAT IT REALLY MEANS: "You all *are* actually cute and gorgeous; you're just not cool enough or dressed right to get into this party."

WHAT THE DOOR BITCH SAYS: "I'm letting you in because you are *you*, and you should remember that."

WHAT IT REALLY MEANS: "You're important or interesting enough to get in, but not important enough to bring any guests."

Continued

meaning "meeting of the waters") and as a teenager migrated to the big city of Vancouver, where he received his unconventional education from "street kids, prostitutes, and drag queens." He soon became involved with an older lover—a rock 'n' roll and travel photographer—and moved to Hawaii with him where he began a career as an actor in TV ads. "I appeared in the first ever commercial for Sony Walkmans in 1979," Derek relates. "I was playing air guitar with a tennis racket, dressed in little tennis shorts." After some TV gigs in Japan and seven years of traveling with his companion, Derek found himself single again and back in Vancouver wondering what to do next. After a stint as a bicycle messenger, Derek decided to move to New York after celebrating New Year's Eve in that city at the end of 1988. "I moved there in the spring of 1989 and went out every single night, dancing to house music at places like Mars and Boy Bar." In the winter of 1989 Derek entered—and won—the Mr. Boy Bar contest. "The prize was one hundred dollars and a job at Boy Bar, which I really needed because I was running out of money. The choice was a bartending job or a doorman job. I knew that bartending was hard work, so I chose the door gig."

He quickly learned "the ropes" from the club's
longtime doorman, Len Whitney, a video artist
known for his penchant for outré leather outfits
and codpieces. "Even though it was only five
dollars to get in, a lot of people were insulted if
they were made to pay," Derek remembers. "Len
taught me which local artists, writers, and performers got in for free, and how to handle all the
egos in a diplomatic way." Another trick he
learned was what to do when the police arrived.

"Boy Bar didn't have a cabaret license, which
meant no dancing, but people danced anyway.
When the cops came by to check on that, I
would push a button by the door that would kill
the power to the turntables downstairs where
Johnny Dynell was DJing. That's when he knew
to put on an Ella Fitzgerald record and by the
time the police made it to the dance floor, everyone was lounging around, smoking cigarettes,
and enjoying Ella." After Boy Bar closed, Derek
had a brief dalliance working as a go-go boy at
Mars and a club housed in an old Con Edison
power plant called The Building. "I was thirty
years old and I knew the go-go gig wasn't a
long-term plan, and that's when I realized the
door job would become my niche career."

Derek then accepted a job offer as the door-

WHAT THE DOOR BITCH SAYS:
"This is just between me and
you: it's really not that cool inside, you don't want to be in
there."

WHAT IT REALLY MEANS: "You're
not cool enough to be in there."

WHAT THE DOOR BITCH SAYS:
"I'm not doing any catalogue
models this season."

WHAT IT REALLY MEANS: "I'm
not letting anyone in who looks
like they got dressed from the
LL Bean or Land's End catalogue."

WHAT THE DOOR BITCH SAYS:
"The board room meeting is
down the street."

WHAT IT REALLY MEANS: "We're
not letting in any conserva-
tively dressed people."

man for the Roxy. "New York was different then, things were more intense . . . you had people wandering the streets in outrageous outfits and in various stages of nudity, and there was a lot of bitchiness and elitism then. And the bitchiness and personal grudges were things we doormen projected onto fairly innocent clubgoers at will . . . in a way it seemed that people *wanted* to be abused," Derek asserts. "There were nights when things would get out of control, when people would spit on me and I would spit back at them . . . one night some guy started cursing me out, and I chased him all the way to the West Side Highway and pushed his face in the snow and told him never to come back to the Roxy again and the whole line applauded. In those days everything was a big show, and doormen were expected to be dramatic. The security who worked with you expected it, they got off on defending you and being your praetorian guard. It's that whole thing about how power corrupts—you're out there in your little fiefdom, your twenty square feet of kingdom, and if you're not self-reflective and conscious of trying to make everyone else feel good, you can start to project your insecurities on people and become abusive and mean."

As his door reign at the Roxy continued on through the 'nineties, Derek began to feel discontented. "I was really unhappy with my job, really miserable, and I was hooked on pills: Vicodins, Percocets, Percodans . . . and I was smoking a lot of weed, doing a bump here and there to round out the recipe . . . so I was often high at work, and it really became a problem."

The years of pill abuse caught up with him on Gay Pride Day in 1997. "I was at the door of the Roxy, there was a huge line stretching around the block, and suddenly I just collapsed on the ground. This big Brazilian security guard lifted me up and held me in place. For the rest of the night I held on to him with one arm and opened the rope for people with the other. I got through that night, but then I was bed-ridden for a month because my liver just gave out from all the pill abuse . . . I'm sure I had hepatitis as well. That's when I decided I needed to clean up and find another way to approach my job." His new approach involved getting to know clubgoers on a deeper, more personal level. "It was no more 'Hi honey, hey baby', it was more really looking into people's eyes, remembering things like who just broke up with who, and who just got a new job, and who was away for awhile, and really connecting with people. You can't do that if you're high."

Derek wasn't the only one who had cleaned up by the late 'nineties. The club scene was also being purged, with crackdowns by the Drug Enforcement Agency, which brought down an entire empire of clubs, including The Limelight, Tunnel, and Palladium. "Suddenly it was all about focusing on rules and regulations and not getting the club in trouble. We had to protect the liquor license because that's the queen bee of any club. If you lose that, you lose the club, and the employees lose their means of support. So part of my job became making sure we kept the drug dealers out of the clubs." Naturally, this new crusade created animosity that went beyond mere spitting and bitchy repartee. "One time a crazy security guard was fired from the Roxy because we found out he was dealing drugs," Derek recalls. "And one night, very late, he drove high-speed down Eighteenth Street the wrong way toward the Roxy and his car plowed through the velvet ropes and stanchions. I threw myself against the side of the building just in time, and he was leaning out the window screaming *'Derek, you motherfucker, I'm gonna kill you!'* And that was the one time I was rewarded by the club owner . . . he put five hundred dollars in my pocket at the end of the night."

As he approaches his sixteenth year of door whoring, Derek is ready to move on. "I'm ready to leave the job . . . I'm not fed up, but I'm satiated. It's been such a great ride, and I feel very privileged and grateful. But the club world doesn't really excite me anymore . . . like when Madonna performed at the club recently. I used to love hanging out with her in front of the club in the early 'nineties, but now it's not such a big deal. I'd rather be on a quiet beach in Brazil with my partner—so that tells me I'm done. I'm approaching my final act, but I have no idea what I'll be doing next."

9.

It's way too late to be this locked inside ourselves.

—INTERPOL

Thomas and his L.A.-based life coach, T. C. Conroy, are sitting on a terrace in New York's West Village, in sweltering, late summer humidity, discussing the Arctic Blast. Thomas—who has just finished a stressful week of producing fashion shows—is dressed in a wrinkled Burberry striped shirt and worn-in Earnest Sewn jeans. T. C. is wearing an aubergine top by Ghost and studded Levis jeans that have been customized with an assortment of patches: Iron Maiden, The Ramones, skulls, Satan, "I Was Born Horny," "Helmet Laws Suck." She emanates both rocker-chic rebellion and focused professionalism. "Thomas, you've outgrown this gig, and you've *really* outgrown this gig when the arctic freeze, that Manhattan winter arctic blast, blows through," T. C. tells him. She fixes her gaze on him through her lavender Gucci sunglasses, which shield her eyes from the midday sunlight bouncing off the terrace's white-painted walls.

"You mean when I get the 'doorman cough'?" Thomas asks,

knowing full well that's exactly what she means. T. C. is specifically referring to the arctic blast of two Decembers ago, when
Thomas had the flu while working the door to the Motherfucker New Year's Eve party.

"To see you, my friend and my client, to see a person that I
care about sick as a dog, standing out in sub-zero temperatures so
he can let a bunch of knuckleheads into a club . . . it's like: *What
are you doing? What are you* doing?" T. C. asks him emphatically.

"That's interesting that you say I've outgrown the doorman
gig, because more and more people who care about me are
telling me that," Thomas replies.

"So the message is loud and clear," T. C. adds.

"Yeah."

A doorman who has a life coach? Why would New York's
top doorman need a life coach? Because that doorman doesn't
want to be a doorman anymore, that's why. "I hit the doorman
glass ceiling over a year ago," Thomas tells her. "I don't want to
be doing this when I'm forty. The career of a doorman doesn't
last forever, and it leads nowhere. Unless I want to start running a nightclub or owning one, there's nowhere else for me to
go. I remember something you told me months ago during a
session, and I quote it all the time: 'I don't want you to be the
person standing outside the party for the rest of your life, I
want you to be an important person *inside* the party.' And
you're right, it has to happen in the next few years."

"You're giving it that much time?" T. C. asks, surprised.

"Right now, yeah," Thomas answers and lets out a groan.

He knows this is not what she wants to hear. He knows that
T. C. realizes he is still holding on to his doorman career, even
though he desperately wants to move on and has been talking
about letting go of the door job in these sessions for the past
year. He breathes in, then breathes out slowly. He stares at the
surface of the round wooden picnic table that the pair is seated
at, which is partially sheltered by a large umbrella. As the afternoon sun dips down and casts its rays on him, Thomas shifts
his chair over into a diminishing patch of shade in an attempt
to escape the oppressive heat.

T. C. has been coaching Thomas on a semiweekly basis for
over a year and a half. They met six years ago through a mutual
friend and bonded over their love of rock 'n' roll and became
friends. T. C. proposed coaching to him because "I could see a
lot of the struggles he was experiencing and I knew that it
wasn't necessary . . . so I wanted to throw him a life preserver."

T. C. began her career as a life coach over four years ago,
when she had an epiphany while driving her Cadillac through
Hollywood. "It was during a time when I was wondering what
I was going to do with my life. I was unemployed, I was lonely,
I was depressed . . . I was really scared and freaked out about
my future—I was at a crossroads. So, as I was turning a corner
on Franklin Avenue, my inner voice spoke to me loud and
clear; it was undeniable. The voice said, 'You are a life coach.'
And from that moment on, I gave it my full attention."

Of course her new career didn't just inexplicably drop down
on her from the heavens. During this time, T. C. was doing a

lot of Kundalini yoga with her friend Jennifer Finch—the bass player from the all-girl punk/metal band L7—and one day Finch dragged her to a class called "Foundations for Elevation." The class is taught by a Sikh, who instructed people on how to build a strong personal foundation for their lives. In addition to the classes, he also conducts private life coaching. T. C. was intrigued and signed up for the one-on-one sessions. "He helped me connect the dots in a way that I had never done in therapy . . . it was really powerful and we were doing great work together. It's what led me to have that moment of clarity on Franklin Avenue. So I immediately signed on for the training program, started connecting to my identity as a coach, and received my coaching license."

Before T. C. discovered life coaching—or, before it discovered her—she worked in the music business for twenty years, spending a lot of time on the road as a band liaison. Rock 'n' roll has been a part of her life since she was ten years old ("I don't want to date myself, but I saw Led Zeppelin"), and when she was twenty-one her boyfriend was the drummer from Guns N' Roses. "I was living in Hollywood working at a record marketing firm and I needed to take my career up a notch, so I told my bosses that I wanted to start traveling. The next thing I knew, I was sitting across a table from David Lee Roth—one of my childhood heroes—being interviewed for a job as his on-tour press coordinator. The interview went on for over three hours, and finally, at the end of it, he asked 'Do you have a boyfriend?' When I replied 'Yes, but he is busy with his own project,' Mr. Roth leaned across the table and said 'Honey, I don't think I want your perfume stinking up my tour bus.'

"I was devastated, but quickly recovered three weeks later when I found myself on a flight to Syracuse to meet up with Peter Gabriel for his *So* tour. That was the beginning of my career as an on-tour liaison. I then went on to work with Joan Jett and the Blackhearts, The Cars, Depeche Mode, Erasure, and The Sugarcubes. Later, I was the front-of-the-house coordinator for the first Lollapalooza and a subsequent one, which featured Metallica. After brief stints working for Def American records and managing a band called Mother Tongue, my rock star marriage—with Depeche Mode singer Dave Gahan—was in a shambles, so I had to choose between domestic life and my career. I chose my marriage and went to England to be with my husband . . . that part of the story took years to play out, and then a few more to get out of the dark room I locked myself into. After the divorce, I then worked for a company where I directed, produced, and starred in streaming Web content for the likes of Ozzfest and the Back Street Boys, but then we got downsized, so I went to Europe for a bit. After a terrible family tragedy, I came up for air from all that, did lots of yoga, and entered the wonderful world of coaching."

It's probably safe to say that someone like Dr. Phil hasn't led such a colorful life, but after such a wild, rocky ride through the music world T. C. thinks she can help bring clarity and serenity to others' lives. "One of the things that separates me from a therapist is that, while a therapist has dedicated a tremendous amount of time and effort to their education, while they were doing that, I was out in the trenches. So who's going to know what's really going on? I've experienced fame, I've experienced wealth—I've had wealth and I've lost wealth—I've experienced different levels of drug addiction, I've experienced recovery, I've experienced loving and losing— all these different things. I know what it's like to be out on the road and have that be my life. I've experienced stage fright and fear of success and all these different things. I've had hands-on experience. So, when it comes to coaching people in creative fields, I fucking *get* it. I understand the struggles of the creative mind. Artists and other creative types package things differently in their heads, and I have an understanding of that thought process because of my life experiences."

So, whereas a rock musician or a writer might be too cynical or skeptical to seek out the services of a square parental figure like Dr. Phil, they may be willing to give someone like T. C. a try, because they can relate to her as a peer—someone they would feel comfortable hanging out with at a Judas Priest re-union gig. "I like to say that I coach the cool kids," says T. C., "and a cool kid might be a twenty-eight-year-old doorman or a fifty-year-old restaurateur. It's the cool kid spirit, and I attract that into my practice."

Because coaching is not therapy, if a client comes to her with issues around addiction or love or family history, T. C. will advise that the person seek out a therapist or a twelve-step program. As an advocate of therapy, she believes that psychoanalysis can work in coordination with life coaching. However, T. C. asserts, "life coaching is not for damaged or broken people. It's for individuals who are functioning at a high level and are ready to notch it up to the next level . . . and then the next level, and then the next level."

"So, you really think the doorman job is a money piece?" The sun has disappeared behind a cloud and T. C. has propped her Gucci sunglasses atop her thick black hair. "Is that the only reason you're holding on to it?"

"I just think, from a financial state, I still need it to get by right now," Thomas replies. "I always think, god I just want that transition into full-time fashion show production and PR to happen, but I'm just trying not to put all my eggs in that transition basket."

A look of skepticism appears on T. C.'s face. For a few moments she's silent. Then she leans in and gives Thomas a serious look. "Thomas, I would like to help you give yourself permission to play a bigger game . . . I know you are holding on to this gig because it supplements your rent, which is wonderful, but if we put our heads together we can find a way for you to pay the bills that will be more in step with who you are now. But there is a disconnect happening here. I think the disconnect, Thomas, is your vision of who you are."

Thomas is silent for several minutes. "I agree," he says finally, although he doesn't sound entirely convincing.

"So that's what we need to work on—your vision of who you are . . . and I believe that's where we bridge the gap from where you are right now to the way you're perceiving yourself right now. When I say playing a bigger game, I'm talking fifty-yard line . . . *pow!* Calvin Klein. Why not? Producing shows in Europe, whatever that looks like for you . . . can you imagine, you turn out a show in Milan and then you have to fly home to do the door at Motherfucker?!"

"It would be kind of a grounding experience . . ."

"It's kind of nonsensical!"

"It's true . . . even though I need the money, I don't like standing outside of parties much anymore," Thomas says quietly. "You know, I've maintained my legendary status in that world, and I'll probably have a little more time in it. . . ."

"You can reinvent yourself in a different way," T. C. says hopefully. "In a bigger way."

"Madonna. For sure. I try to bring her into every coaching session," Thomas laughs.

"I love her. I try to work her into each of my sessions, too. I support that . . . that bitch runs a good schedule!"

"That was one of the biggest lessons you ever taught me, when you talked about her living a tightly scheduled life . . . and there's nothing wrong with that! At first I said, 'I don't want to *be* like Madonna,' and you said 'You know Thomas, she's a very successful person.' "

"You can do worse in life than Madonna . . . and I'm glad she's here with us right now." T. C. gently knocks on the table as if making contact with the blonde quasi-deity. "Alright, so I'll hold that vision for you, Thomas."

"Thank you."

Thomas rolls over in bed and the loud crunch of a plastic Heaven Scent fudge cookie container wakes him up. He groans and looks at the clock: three P.M. After a long night of dealing with pushy hipsters and vain fashionistas at the door to a party at the Maritime Hotel, Thomas plans on staying in bed all day—three P.M. is way too early to start a Saturday. The phone rings and he grabs his Marc Jacobs military jacket that he flung at the foot of the mattress early this morning and pulls it over his head. "Hey Thomas, it's Skip, are you there?" Skip, a low-maintenance friend, is one of the few people that Thomas would consider speaking to now. "Oh, maybe you're out . . . I'm gonna try calling you on your 'crackberry'—" Thomas reaches for the phone. "Hi, doll," he says sleepily.

"Oh god, did I wake you up? I'm so sorry. Rough night?" Skip asks.

"Just another looong night at the Maritime. And I feel like I'm getting sick again." Thomas reaches for a box of tissues that is perched atop a pile of dirty socks.

"Maybe I should bring you some chicken soup and an echinacea-wheat grass smoothie. I just wanted to tell you I saw *America's Next Top Model* the other night and they showed footage of the winner, Niema, walking in the Christopher

Deane fashion show. Didn't you produce that show during the last fashion week?"

Thomas sits up and a hint of perkiness enters his voice. "Oh cool, you saw that? Yeah, I produced that show with my friend Max. We were really happy with the way it turned out."

"It looked like a really fun show, you did a great job," Skip tells him.

"Thank you! Yeah, we'll be working with them again next season, they're great clients." Suddenly Thomas is up and has abandoned the prospect of going back to sleep. As he continues talking to Skip, he goes into multitasking mode, sits in front of his computer—which he forgot to shut down the night before—and begins scanning his list of new e-mails. "Skip, let's meet for coffee tomorrow and catch up, okay? I see a few e-mails here from some potential fashion clients who I've been chasing for a long time now."

"Sounds like a plan, call me when you wake up tomorrow." Skip hangs up and Thomas gets to work answering his e-mails. *Time to notch things up to the next level,* he thinks to himself.

DOOR BITCH GLOSSARY

A IS FOR THE A LIST. Also known as VIPs, members of the A List are at the top of the nightlife food chain and their existence is one of the main reasons the velvet ropes are necessary. A good doorman will be able to spot them right away, but because of the A Listers' proclivity toward changing their hair/signature style/noses/faces, etc., sometimes they blend in with hoi polloi. (Caroline Kennedy was once neglected outside of Studio 54 because she was hiding under a Texas Rangers cap.) A Listers include but are not limited to: young rock stars, old rock legends, known fashion world denizens (Karl Lagerfeld plus entourage—yes; Fran Drescher's seamstress—no), Hollywood actors, It Girls/Boys, important members of the media, cultural icons, some cultural critics, members of any royal family, socialites, trendy politicos, some best-selling authors, and the doorman's mother.

B IS FOR BOUNCER. Also known as "member of the security team," this big bruiser supplies the brawn that works in tandem with the doorman's razor-sharp brain. He is the praetorian guard that stands watch over the door bitch's tiny, roped-in fiefdom. Essential to the smooth operation of any nightclub, the bouncer is always at the ready to back up the door bitch's decisions, eject unruly rabble-rousers, and check IDs.

C IS FOR CRAZY PEOPLE. If nightclubs were only patronized by well-behaved, mentally stable, upstanding citizens, they wouldn't be very much fun, would they? Crazy people—drunken loonies, obsessed fans, pathological party crashers, and sociopathic promoters—will always add plenty of spice to even the dullest downtown shindigs.

D IS FOR DRINK TICKET. Like Willie Wonka's golden ticket, the drink ticket, which entitles the bearer to one free drink, is a pass into a loopy, magical realm—that is, if you can procure enough of them. If you're a friend of the doorman, a VIP, or a jaded journalist who is in need of social lubrication, chances are you can score some drink tickets upon entrance into the club. However, be warned: When the door bitch says there are no more drink tickets, he's not kidding—so don't ask him again. **D Is also for Derek Neen.** This long-time velvet ropes doctor has been entertaining and antagonizing hapless club-goers with his door-side manner for over fifteen years.

E IS FOR EGO. A nightclubber without an ego is like a pop star without a publicist, but you would be well-advised to check your hubris *before* you get to the door—because the door bitch doesn't have time for it. Unless you're Nicole Kidman, Martha Stewart, or Tony Blair, save the attitude for the deli worker who screws up your pastrami sandwich order.

F IS FOR FAKE ID. No matter how cleverly you think you've doctored your driver's license, if you're an underage phony, the door bitch will sniff you out faster than you can say "juvie court."

G IS FOR GUEST LIST. Getting your name on a guest list for the first time is a rite of passage for any ambitious club-goer; being on them all the time is proof that you've "arrived." Whether your name on the guest list excludes you from paying an entrance fee or is a prerequisite for getting in at all, one thing is for certain: If you're on the guest list, you're better than everyone else waiting in line (or that's what you'll keep telling yourself).

H IS FOR H & M. This emporium of low-priced clothing rolls out the latest trends, like McDonald's cheeseburgers, on a weekly basis. H & M is an ideal place for hipsters on a budget to throw together a look that will increase their chances of get-ting past the door bitch. This shopping expedition should not be looked at lightly—while well-to-do trendoids sip champagne at the Dior boutique, H & M shoppers risk being trampled to death when the latest thrifty concoctions from Karl Lagerfeld or Stella McCartney are wheeled out.

IS FOR I. As in "Don't you know who I am?" or "I know I'm on the guest list" or "I need more drink tickets." People in New York City, even those who don't go out to clubs, love using the letter *I* almost as much as they love using the royal "we."

IS FOR JUDGING. One thing you will need to get used to if you enjoy going out to clubs is being judged. From your hairdo down to your shoes, the door bitch will mercilessly scan every square inch of your body with laserlike precision, deciding whether you're worthy enough to pass through the ropes. Try not to let this discourage you from going out: make your best effort, and when you get to the door just keep repeating to yourself, "It's only a nightclub, it's only a nightclub. . . ."

IS FOR KENNY KENNY. One of New York's original door bitches, this androgynous work of art has, over the course of his eighteen-year career, gone from ferocious hellhound to repentant sprite.

IS FOR LATE. As any seasoned nightcrawler knows, being late is the right time to arrive at any club, when the party is pumping and you can make your proper entrance. However, late is something the doorman can never be—if the evening begins and the bouncers are left stranded at the ropes without the aid of the door bitch's crowd-control skills and caustic tongue, things could get very ugly.

M IS FOR MARC BENECKE. As the former doorman of the most famous club in history—Studio 54—Marc Benecke is the godfather of the velvet ropes. While Bianca, Halston, and Andy were shuttled into this mighty disco Valhalla night after night, Marc kept the polyester-clad clods and unfabulous flops out.

N IS FOR NO. As in, "No, you can't come in," "No, I don't see your name on the list," and "No, Paris Hilton is not here." No is one of the door bitch's favorite words, and more times than not "no" really means no.

O IS FOR OLD SCHOOL. Old school refers to the method that doormen like Thomas utilize when they work the door. While the criteria at many new clubs involves admitting patrons who are able to afford expensive bottles of alcohol, the old school style involves selecting patrons based on their personal style, overall originality, quirky beauty, alluring ugliness, or interesting work credentials (DJ, trendy makeup artist, up-and-coming fashion designer, struggling performer, sublebrity, etc.).

P IS FOR PRIVATE PARTY. In the club world, a private party can range from the unveiling of new designer swizzle stick to a bat mitzvah hosted by Madonna—invite-only or at the doorman's discretion. However a private party is also a standard fib that door bitches cite when they just don't feel like letting you in to a nonprivate event. **P Is also for Page Six.** Page Six is the vicious and delicious gossip column that has been appearing in the *New York Post* for decades, and where denizens of the door bitch's world are often written up. Anyone with even an ounce of ambition or ego wakes up every morning filled with a mixture of fear and hope over the notion that they may have been mentioned in Page Six.

Q IS FOR QUEENS. Because a nightclub without a token number of decorative drag queens is like a bordello without married politician customers.

R IS FOR ROCK STARS. From quasi has-beens like Mark McGrath to timeless icons like Mick Jagger, rock stars always get VIP treatment from the door bitch.

S IS FOR STUDIO 54. Because sooner or later, you're going to run into a seasoned disco dervish wearing a stretched-out pair of gold lamé Fiorucci jeans who will shake his cane at you and shout "It was so much better at Studio!" **S Is also for Sub-**

lebrity. Without these small-time stars and their big-time egos, the club scene would be a boring place indeed.

T IS FOR THOMAS ONORATO. Even if you never heard of this famous doorman until you picked up this book, we're certain you'll be dropping his name at every club, bar, and bingo hall from Albuquerque to Liverpool.

U IS FOR UNLISTED PHONE NUMBER. Because doormen are often besieged with guest list requests, they need to have an unlisted phone number. However, even an unlisted phone number isn't protection against the legions of club land freeloaders and C-List nuisances, because eventually many of them will track down the phone number of every doorman in town. As a result, many doormen find themselves changing their numbers on a regular basis. If the day comes when they leave the doorman profession, the phone becomes eerily silent. "I used to have to change my number every three months," Marc Benecke has said. "After Studio closed, the calls, invites, and Christmas presents stopped coming. And now I only change my number every three years."

V IS FOR VELVET ROPES. When they're not made of velvet, sometimes the ropes are vinyl and sometimes they're virtual . . . but wherever a door bitch stands guard, this iconic nightlife force field will always be in place.

W IS FOR WORK A LOOK! Whether that look is a plastic lobster and a baguette tied to your head or just a cute skirt and vintage tee, if you want to get past the door bitch work it, boys and girls, work it.

X IS FOR PROJECT X. In the dark ages before Web 'zines, photo blogs, and MySpace.com, there was a seminal magazine published by club kids between the late 'eighties and early 'nineties called *Project X*. A key influence in Thomas's development as a door bitch, *Project X* published outrageous photos and stories from the club days of yore—before clubgoers were spoiled by the instant ego-satisfaction of digital technology.

Y IS FOR YES. "Yes" is the word that club people want to hear the most: "Yes, you can come in," "Yes, you're on the list," "Yes, I have drink tickets," "Yes dear, you look skinnier than Nicole Richie."

Z IS FOR ZOMBIES. Often outside the ropes, a disturbing mob mentality overcomes people who are basically well-behaved in daylight hours. Even after the doorman tells them the list is closed, the club is full to capacity, "Everyone, please go home!," crowds of party people will ignore these decrees and continue to ominously close in on the velvet ropes and the doorman, like deaf and dumb Zombies from a bad B-movie.

GLENN BELVERIO is a writer who lives in New York City.

THOMAS ONORATO is a doorman and public relations consultant who lives in New York City. His public relations clients range from nightlife to lifestyle, and he has produced numerous fashion shows during New York Fashion Week.

PHOTO by Torkil Gudnason

GROOMING by William Murphy

HAIR by Johnny Gaita

Shirt and vest by J. Lindeberg; Jeans by Earnest Sewn; Chainmail bracelet by Michael Schmidt

T-Shirt by H & M; Jeans by Helmut Lang